Sir Thomas Wyatt

Twayne's English Authors Series

Arthur F. Kinney, Editor
University of Massachusetts, Amherst

TEAS 475

Sir Thomas Wyatt

By Stephen Merriam Foley

Brown University

Twayne Publishers
A Division of G. K. Hall & Co. • *Boston*

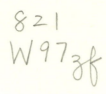

Sir Thomas Wyatt
Stephen Merriam Foley

Copyright 1990 by G. K. Hall & Co.
All rights reserved.
Published by Twayne Publishers
A division of G. K. Hall & Co.
70 Lincoln Street
Boston, Massachusetts 02111

Copyediting supervised by Barbara Sutton.
Book production by Janet Z. Reynolds.
Book design by Barbara Anderson.
Typeset in 11 pt. Garamond by Compositors Corporation, Cedar Rapids, Iowa.

Printed on permanent/durable acid-free paper
and bound in the United States of America.

First published 1990.
10 9 8 7 6 5 4 3 2 1

Library of Congress Cataloging-in-Publication Data

Foley, Stephen Merriam.
    Sir Thomas Wyatt / Stephen Merriam Foley.
        p.   cm. — (Twayne's English authors series : TEAS 475)
    Includes bibliographical references.
    ISBN 0–8057–6992–7
    1. Wyatt, Thomas, Sir. 1503?–1542—Criticism and interpretation.
I. Title.   II. Series.
PR2404.F57   1990
821'.2—dc20   89–77339
                                                                          CIP

For Mary Jo

Contents

Editor's Note

Sir Thomas Wyatt has long been considered the premiere poet in the long reign of Henry VIII and one of three major English poets in the first half of the sixteenth century; as a pioneer, he introduced to England the Petrarchan sonnet, the verse epistle, and the form for penitential psalms. Now a new pioneer, Stephen Merriam Foley, applies the latest critical techniques to Wyatt's work—originally unsigned and surviving in scattered manuscripts, some with several layers of composition and revision—to learn how, under heterogeneous historical conditions, Wyatt wrote his work and how, under present conditions, we may be enabled to read and understand them. Foley is not here concerned simply with what Wyatt's poems may mean but, more fundamentally and far more significantly, how Tudor culture allowed these poems to come into being and meaning. The result is a strikingly original, compelling, and seminal study of Sir Thomas Wyatt, of early Renaissance English poetry, and of critical understanding that should revitalize our study of poetry in general and Wyatt's work in particular.

Arthur F. Kinney

About the Author

Stephen Merriam Foley is an associate professor of English at Brown University. He received his undergraduate education at Brown and pursued graduate studies at Yale, where he received a Ph.D. in English in 1979. He taught English at Yale and served as research editor for the Yale edition of *The Works of St. Thomas More* before returning to Brown in 1982. He is coeditor with Clarence Miller of Thomas More's *Answer to the Poisoned Book,* More's reply to a Zwinglian pamphlet against the doctrine of the real presence (volume 11 in the Yale edition); he is coauthor with Joseph Gordon of a handbook on style and usage, *Conventions and Choices;* and he has also published articles on English and continental literature in the sixteenth century.

Preface

Since the beginning of this century Thomas Wyatt has eclipsed his literary successor, Henry Howard, earl of Surrey, as the most widely read poet of early sixteenth-century England. His contemporaries and later sixteenth-century readers recognized Wyatt as one who had enabled the new "renaissance" style in English letters. In Surrey's words, he possessed "a hand that taught what might be said in rhyme." This study attempts to use an awareness of the ways in which the human subject is positioned by his or her culture in order to encourage a problematic historical awareness in our readings of Wyatt's work. Emphasizing the material conditions of reading and writing, it reexamines the documentary sources of Wyatt's life and letters, seeking what their rhetorical strategies conceal as well as what "facts" they record. Rather than ask what Wyatt's works mean, this study tries to open up the question of how Tudor culture allowed these works to come to meaning. What were the heterogeneous historical conditions under which the hand of Thomas Wyatt wrote his poems and through which they must be read? In thinking about this project, I have been grateful for the work of Thomas Greene and Stephen Greenblatt, who provide the most challenging recent commentaries on Wyatt; I have also drawn widely and silently on some of the assumptions of recent work on early modern English culture by such historians as Catherine Belsey, Jonathan Crewe, Jonathan Dollimore, Margaret Ferguson, Alastair Foxe, Jonathan Goldberg, John Guy, David Loades, Louis Adrian Montrose, Alan Sinfield, Peter Stallybrass, David Starkey, Gary Waller, and Frank Whigham. I am grateful for the full annotations in the edition of Wyatt's poems by Ronald Rebholz, as well as for the work of the pioneers of twentieth-century Wyatt scholarship: Agnes Foxwell, E. M. W. Tillyard, E. K. Chambers, Hyder Rollins, Kenneth Muir, and Patricia Thomson. I am ever amazed by the perspicuity of the irascible H. A. Mason and the foresightedness of Raymond Southall, who perhaps first and best among the contemporary readers of Wyatt have tried to historicize our appreciation. Raymond Southall first unwrapped the many stories inscribed in the Devonshire manuscript, and my reading of the Wyatt manuscripts would not have been possible without the example he set and the assiduous textual scholarship of Richard Harrier, Ruth Hughey, and Joost Daalder. Mason's new edition of selected poems by Wyatt came to my attention too late for me to make use of it. I have added it to the bibliography. Like all students of Wyatt, I continue to stand in awe of the scholarship of the first modern edition of Wyatt's and Surrey's works, produced by George Frederick Nott in 1815. I am grateful to my Twayne editors, Arthur Kinney, Janet Reynolds, and Barbara Sutton. Whenever I write about the Tudor period I reflect on what good fortune I have had to study and work with scholars like Sears Jayne, Thomas Greene, Louis Martz, Clarence Miller, Michael Putnam, Andrew Sabol, and Richard Sylvester. I still hear early Tudor texts in Richard Sylvester's voice. Jonathan Goldberg has been more than generous in his encouragement and support, as has my old friend Richard Marius. David Kastan and Peter Stallybrass became my new friends in helping me with this project. At Brown I have been grateful for the assistance of friends like William Keach, Elizabeth Kirk, Roger Henkle, John Murchek, Geoffrey Russom, Robert Scholes, and Walter Davis, who first suggested I write this book. Coppélia Kahn and Karen Newman made me finish it. My children, Nicholas and Benjamin, know when to leave me alone and when not to. Of course, this book is for Mary Jo with all my love.

Stephen Merriam Foley

Brown University

Chronology

1503   Thomas Wyatt born at Allington Castle, near Maidstone, Kent, son of Henry Wyatt, master of the king's jewels, keeper of the exchange, and assayer of the money and coinage, and Anne, daughter of John Skinner of Reigate, Surrey.

1509   Henry Wyatt made knight of the Bath at the coronation of Henry VIII; retains all offices under the new king and receives frequent grants of land in reward for his services.

1516   Thomas Wyatt serves as sewer (table servant) extraordinary at the christening of Princess Mary.

1519   Henry Wyatt is named treasurer of the king's chamber.

1520   Thomas Wyatt marries Elizabeth Brooke, daughter of George, Lord Cobham, whose principal manor abuts Allington. Wyatt later (ca. 1525–26) repudiates his wife for adultery.

1521   Thomas Wyatt's only legitimate son is born and named Thomas.

1524   Thomas Wyatt serves as esquire of the body to Henry VIII; is named clerk of the king's jewels 21 October and serves until 1530; participates in mock battle and tournament during Christmas revels at Greenwich.

1526   Accompanies Sir Thomas Cheney to the French court to offer Francis I congratulations of his release after the disastrous Battle of Pavia and to negotiate the position of England in relation to the Holy League of Cognac.

1527   Accompanies Sir John Russell on an embassy to the papal court in the midst of the imperial invasion of Italy; visits Ferrara, Bologna, and Florence; is captured by the Spanish and ransomed; leaves Rome days before it is sacked by imperial troops.

1528   Presents his translation of Plutarch's *Quiet of Mind* to Queen Catherine as a new year's gift; Richard Pynson issues a printed edition.

1529   Named high marshall of Calais 26 September–22 November 1530; licensed to import wine and woad.

1532   Appointed justice of the peace in Essex; his debts to the king are included on Cromwell's list of desperate bills; is possibly among the courtiers who accompany the king and Anne Boleyn to Calais for a meeting with Francis I.

1533 Stands in for his father as chief sewer at the coronation of Queen Anne 1 June.

1534 Is briefly committed to the Fleet Prison after a brawl with some sergeants of London in which one of the sergeants was killed; licensed to have twenty men in his livery and to raise and command men for war throughout Kent.

1535 Named high steward of the abbey of West Malling, Kent; knighted 18 March (Easter Day); granted a leasehold on Aryngden Park, Yorkshire.

1536 Arrested 5 May after the May Day jousts and imprisoned in the Tower among those charged with adultery with Queen Anne; is still in the Tower when Anne is beheaded; released by mid-June to his father's custody at Allington following his father's and Cromwell's intervention. Henry Wyatt entertains Henry VIII at Allington 31 July. Thomas Wyatt named steward of Connisborough Castle, Yorkshire, and sheriff of Kent; raises 350 men for service in the campaign against the northern uprising called the Pilgrimage of Grace. Henry Wyatt dies 10 November. Thomas Wyatt the younger marries Jane Hawte, daughter and co-heir of Sir William Hawte of Bourne, Kent.

1537 Granted livery of his father's lands in February; dispatched to the imperial court where he serves for the next two years, charged with the impossible task of improving strained relations between England and the Holy Roman Empire; stops in Paris, Lyons, Avignon, Barcelona, Saragossa; addresses two letters of advice to his son; at Barbastro in Spain composes "Of Carthage he." Some of Wyatt's lyrics appear in a printed collection, *The Court of Venus,* published ca. 1537–39.

1538 Wyatt is joined on his embassy (now in Nice) by Edmund Bonner and Simon Heynes as Charles V, Francis I, and the pope gather to work out a new alliance in April. Cromwell writes of the failure of Wyatt's friends to look after his interests at home. Wyatt returns to England briefly in June in order to confer at court; visits with his mistress, Elizabeth Darrell, at Allington; follows imperial court to Spain; charges by Bonner against Wyatt investigated by Cromwell and suppressed; involved in conspiracy to assassinate Reginald Cardinal Pole.

1539 Leaves Toledo to return to England, commemorating departure in

"Tagus farewell." Is again in November sent to follow the imperial court as it travels through France and the Burgundian territories.

1540   Returns to England in May. Cromwell arrested. Witnesses Cromwell's execution 28 July.

1541   Arrested for treason 17 January on Bonner's old charges; writes a "declaration" of his innocence and a formal oration in his defense; charges dismissed without trial after a confession; is made captain of three hundred light cavalry in April; writes a will 12 June naming his son Thomas his principal heir and leaving some properties to Elizabeth Darrell and his illegitimate son Francis.

1542   Is given offices formerly belonging to Thomas Culpepper, recently executed for adultery with Catherine Howard; exchanges of property with the king give him possession of extensive properties surrounding Montagu priory as well as other properties in Kent and Somerset; is named high steward of the royal manor of Maidstone in Kent; is named captain of a galley and vice admiral of the fleet for war against France; is dispatched to Falmouth to greet imperial ambassador; collapses and dies at Sherborne, Dorset, 11 October. Elegies are published by John Leland, the king's antiquary, and by Henry Howard, earl of Surrey.

1549   *Certain Psalms* published.

1557   Extensive selection of Wyatt's poems published in *Songs and Sonnets* ("Tottel's Miscellany").

Chapter One
Reading Thomas Wyatt's Hand

The life of Thomas Wyatt is written in manuscript. From the first record of his name—the twelve-year-old "T. Wyet" is listed as sewer extraordinary to Henry VIII for the christening of Princess Mary in 1516—through the record of his burial in the great church at Sherborne, Dorset, on 11 October 1542,[1] the life of Sir Thomas Wyatt is inscribed—incompletely, sporadically, partially, inconsistently—in the many hands of early Tudor society: the racing secretary hand of diplomatic, military, and household correspondence; the dense chancery hand of legal documents; the proud humanist italics advertising the new learning; the playful and reckless, often untutored hands of courtiers passing notes like schoolchildren under the master's eyes; the deliberate hand of a man who signs himself with a monogram "T.V." (for a Latinized "Thomas Viatus") as he makes new entries and changes in the small folio codex where for a time he collected poems.

On some seventy folio leaves at the beginning of this manuscript, now Egerton MS. 2711 in the British Library,[2] poems appear in several sixteenth-century hands, set in the center of the pages with generous margins. Many are lyrics: ballades, rondeaux, and songs in the Anglo-French style that had enjoyed currency for several generations at the English court. Many are Petrarchan sonnets, a form new to English poetry in the early sixteenth century. Three are neoclassicizing Horatian satires, also a generic novelty in English; others are classical translations or imitations. Some are epigrams. One sequence is a translation of the seven penitential psalms. These poems and others attributed to Wyatt appear elsewhere—in other manuscript collections and in the widely circulated anthology, *Songs and Sonnets*, issued by the printer Richard Tottel in 1557 and often called "Tottel's Miscellany." Although many of these sources provide reliable texts and credible attributions, only in the Egerton manuscript is there evidence of Wyatt's own hand for poems that were "his," and even here the evidence of authorship is uncertain because its conventions are not entirely recoverable. Only a few poems in Egerton are entirely in Wyatt's own hand. In some he has simply made changes in texts entered by other hands, presumably those of secretaries, perhaps signing these poems "Tho." to signal his approval of the change—or

1

perhaps the "Tho." was added later as an attribution by an intimate of the family.[3] Despite these uncertainties, it is clear that Wyatt was responsible for the poems in this manuscript, and the manuscript is thus unique in this period as a collection of lyric poems by a single author. Most lyrics in the fifteenth and early sixteenth century remained anonymous, and they were not generally compiled in manuscripts for their own sake. Lyrics of course were sometimes attracted to the oeuvre of Chaucer or of Lydgate. But only in the collections of poems in French and English attributed to Charles d'Orleans is there a substantial body of lyrics by a given "poet."[4]

The Egerton manuscript is also unique as being in any sense a working volume.[5] But the poems are hard to read. The manuscript has been cut up. Some of the original leaves are missing, others have been repaired or replaced. It was rebound in the early nineteenth century. Its pages are dense with layers of inscription. Changes have been entered, words and punctuation added and deleted, lines cancelled, titles and attributions added. Traces of different inks, pens, and hands mark the pages and compete for attention. On the leaves at the end of the codex, following the collection of poems, a late sixteenth-century hand has copied *sententiae* from Latin and Greek authors; another late-Tudor hand has copied a recipe on the blank space of folio 117 recto. And a seventeenth-century hand has filled in almost every other available space on the blank leaves at the beginning and the end of the codex and on the margins of occupied pages, sometimes crossing out poems to mark them off from the new text or turning the manuscript upside down to write, putting the scraps to use for religious and scientific jottings and for mathematical calculations. There are also, a modern editor notes, "innumerable scribbles by hands that are not worth mentioning."[6]

Thomas Wyatt's own hand can be identified in the Egerton manuscript because it is well known from another important Wyatt manuscript collection, a volume of letters also in the British Library, Harleian MS. 282.[7] Almost all of these letters are official correspondence written by Wyatt or received by him while abroad on diplomatic missions. Some of the documents are in his hand; others are copies made by secretaries and authorized by Wyatt. All undoubtedly are Wyatt's personal copies—drafts or second copies of documents he sent back to court. These letters have been carefully preserved. Wyatt himself must have kept the collection intact; it was the record of his official service, saved to justify his actions if he were challenged—as indeed it was used when he was in danger of being placed on trial for treason in 1541.[8] This collection was intended to record Wyatt's activities for official posterity, and its integrity has not been jeopardized by those who preserved the collection after; indeed it may have been treated as a memorial volume.

As contemporary literary history recovers Thomas Wyatt as a canonical author of the early modern era, the Egerton manuscript serves as the focus for the difficult scholarly problem of identifying the poems that Thomas Wyatt wrote, of determining the poems that are in the broadest sense "from his hand"—a problem on which few scholars agree. The Egerton manuscript is by no means the only authority (nor an uncomplicated one), and the attributions of other sources must also be considered. For the biographer or the political historian, the Harleian collection does much to establish the record of his official duties, the "hand" that Wyatt exercised in the Tudor court and administration. But both these important scholarly enterprises are part of a larger problem in cultural history, for one reads Thomas Wyatt's hand as his own only in relation to other hands, and one can understand the Wyatt manuscripts only by understanding the circumstances in which they are implicated.

How can one read the ways in which the hand of an individual human agent was written in the shifting texts of early sixteenth-century English culture? How is "T.V." the authorial signature related to the many other ways in which "Thomas Wyatt" was inscribed by his culture? How was the identity of "Thomas Wyatt" constituted? What did it mean to "sign" a poem? What kind of work did authorship perform? What were the conditions of authorship for an ambitious and successful courtier like Thomas Wyatt? How is the authorial hand of the Egerton manuscript ("T.V.") the same or different from the official hand of the Harleian manuscript where "Thomas Wyat" (he never used the double "t") also signed his name? What is named by "Thomas Wyatt" in documents outside the sphere "authenticated" by "T.V." or by "Thomas Wyat"? How do these two manuscripts, kept so differently by their author and by posterity, share common histories? How does the "Huyot" who figures so strongly in the dispatches of the Spanish ambassador relate to the "Wyat" who sent letters to his own king from Spain? How can we best read the historical conditions under which these documents, letters and poems alike, were produced and under which they produced the life of Thomas Wyatt?

The Egerton and Harleian manuscripts can in one sense be seen as "authentic" sources for the study of Thomas Wyatt's life. And indeed the many stories of Thomas Wyatt's life circulate again and again through these two manuscripts. But they are not authentic simply because they were written "by" him, or because they reveal "him," or even because they embody a single, coherent narrative of "his" life. They do not, and they will not answer all my questions. They are authentic because they are places where one can read the heterogeneous conditions under which many different hands—Wyatt's own and those of others—defined the fields of human action in which he lived. These two manuscripts are surely "authentic." But curiously they can be "authenticated," made valuable as tools of historical inquiry, only when their strict "authority" as sources validated by the mere signature of their "author" is opened up and the words of "Thomas Wyatt" are exposed as sites for the circulation of the shifting, versatile, contradictory discourses that constituted his culture.

Fables: Sons and Fathers

Let us begin this life of Sir Thomas Wyatt with a source of doubtful "authenticity": the anonymous chronicle compiled from family lore several generations after Wyatt's death and reported at length in articles by John Bruce in the *Gentleman's Magazine* of 1850.[9] I am drawn in particular to two animal stories. They are merry tales, typical of the stories that the men and women of early sixteenth-century England enjoyed telling about one another, and they have a cultural authority of their own, apart from the documentary credibility of archival sources like court records or baptismal entries. One, the story of a loyal cat and its loyal master, concerns the imprisonment of Thomas Wyatt's father, Sir Henry Wyatt, an adherent of Henry VII who advanced in his king's service and rose to even higher office at court under Henry VIII. The second, about Thomas Wyatt, a young lion, a greyhound, and Henry VIII, suggests the dangerous negotiations through which youthful ambition almost bites the hand that feeds it and sons prove themselves different from their fathers.

Sir Henry Wyatt had been born into a family of prosperous landholders long and safely resident in Yorkshire.[10] Little evidence indicates what circumstances brought this young provincial Yorkshireman to the field in the dynastic wars of the later fifteenth century, but many stories circulate about his loyalty to Henry Tudor, for it was through Henry Wyatt's service to the ultimately victorious Lancastrian earl of Richmond that the Wyatt family gained entrance into the powerful circle around the throne. The stories that get repeated most often about Henry Wyatt concern his long imprisonment as a vassal of his defeated lord. Thomas Wyatt wrote to his own son that his father had been imprisoned in Scotland "two years and more" during the years before the Tudor victory at Bosworth Field in 1485 (most likely he was caught up in the unsuccessful Buckingham's Rebellion of 1483). The family chronicle fleshes out the story of his imprisonment (there are supposed to have been several periods of captivity) with witty literary "examples" of his loyalty under duress. Henry Wyatt is supposed, in the account of one stay in prison, to have been submitted to torture by Richard III in person:

"Wyatt," said the tyrant, "why art thou such a fool? Thou servest for moonshine in the water. Thy master is a beggarly fugitive. Forsake him and become mine. I can re-ward thee, and I swear unto thee, I will." "Sir," was his answer, "If I had first chosen you for my master, thus faithful would I have been to you, if you should have needed it; but the Earl, poor and unhappy though he be, is my master, and no discourage-ment or allurement shall ever drive or draw me from him, by God's grace."

Such cool, uncritical loyalty provides exquisite credentials for the servant of the crown, all effected in the name of God's grace. And God's providence, the same chronicler reveals, in turn favored the imprisoned Henry Wyatt with the services of an obliging cat:

He was imprisoned often; once in a cold and narrow tower, where he had neither bed to lie on, nor clothes sufficient to warm him, nor meat for his mouth. He had starved there had not God, who sent a crow [raven?] to feed his prophet, sent this his and his country's martyr a cat both to feed and warm him. It was his own relation unto them from whom I had it. A cat came one day down into the dungeon unto him, and as it were offered herself unto him. He was glad of her, laid her in his bosom to warm him, and by making much of her, won her love. After this she would come every day unto him divers times, and when she could get one, bring him a pigeon. He complained to his keeper of his cold and short fare. The answer was, "he durst not better it." "But," said Sir Henry, "if I can provide any, will you promise to dress it for me?" "I may well enough," said he, the keeper, "you are safe for that matter"; and being urged again, promised him and kept his promise, dressed for him from time to time such pigeons as his accator [purveyor] the cat provided for him.[11]

Here are the operations of a domestic and practical divine providence, al-ways there when needed, or at least supposed to have been there when things worked out as one had hoped. But the story is above all a fable of the perils and rewards of personal loyalty, and there is indeed an atavistic element of chivalric romance here. To be sure, Henry Wyatt was a loyal vassal. While still a young man in the 1490s he was employed to bring permission to Scots rebels; he led the battle against Scots incursions as captain of Carlisle and as-sisted in Ireland during the years of Perkin Warbeck's rebellion; he was also among the leaders in the fight at Blackheath against Cornish rebels protest-ing the subsidies for the Scots wars.[12] He would serve again in battle as a member of the advance guard at Calais in the glorious landing in France in 1513.[13] He received, in addition to the emoluments of his many royal appointments, an additional £20 a year in recognition of his imprisonment in Scotland.[14] But his most important service to Henry VII and later to Henry VIII (and the efficient cause of Henry VIII's renewal of the "Scots" pension in 1514) was fiscal and administrative, not military. In Ireland in 1495 he audited the accounts of the English armies. His most important task in preparing for the French campaigns was as commissioner of naval supplies. Henry Wyatt came into importance as *noblesse de la robe*—or, to be more precise, of the purse, for he made his career in the household, supervising some of the principal working accounts of the king. By 1486 Henry Wyatt was named clerk of the king's jewels (under an absentee master of the jewel house); in 1488, clerk of the mint. He was later named master of the jewel house, keeper of the exchange, and assayer of coinage,[15] becoming a member of the council and esquire of the body for Henry VII.[16] And he was amply rewarded, with annual stipends, of course, but, more important, with lands that were the start of the Wyatt family's rich holdings in Kent and elsewhere. This old war story, then, encodes the risks and rewards of a far different kind of service, casting the administrative and political acumen of a "modern" accountant and bureaucrat as the fealty of a warrior in the field. It suppresses and masks the social change that the rise of men like Wyatt—neither clerics nor nobles—in royal service represented.[17] And, like most stories about people and animals, it tells more than it ought to.

This memorable merry tale plays with taboo and titillation and the mystique of male empowerment in the unabashed "availability" of the cat (this was no tom) to the "master" who "won her love." And alongside the moral of the fable (God looks after his own loyal servants and the king's) it inscribes the willing complicity of the keeper ("You are safe for that matter") and the predatory instincts and accomplishments of the otherwise cuddly and obliging cat. This is a story written for and about people who understand the vicious delicacy of the personal politics of court and faction. Perhaps Sir Henry's lifelong devotion to cats, as the chronicle in the same passage claims—("for this would ever make much of cats, as other men will of their spaniels or hounds"), is not altogether benign. In affecting the love of cats—he is said to have had his portrait painted holding a cat as other men would a favorite dog—Henry Wyatt presents a studious contrast to the careless aristocrat indulging thoughtlessly in the pleasures of the hunt. And besides, cats are such wonderfully domesticated hunters. Cats nap, and wait, and cuddle, on your lap or in your bosom, until they pounce.

Like this cat story, the story of young Thomas Wyatt and the lion is also about domesticated violence, and it too bristles beyond and outgrows its moral:

He brought up at Allington Castle a lion's whelp and an Irish greyhound in which he took much delight; and their manner was in his absence to attend his home-coming at the gate or hall-door; and many times there they met him and with great joy entertained him. But at length when the lion's whelp grew into courage and heat, instead of friendly welcome, it ran roaring upon him, and flew fiercely into his bosom, and had certainly destroyed him but for the greyhound, who, coming after the lion, was as soon in his neck as he in his master's bosom, and with his teeth pulled him on his back, until Sir Thomas Wyat, in a most present and undaunted courage, drew forth his rapier and ran it into the rebel's heart. When he afterwards went to court and there distinguished himself by his free and daring spirit, Henry VIII, who had heard of this memorable incident, remarked of him, "Oh, he can tame lions!"[18]

In some ways, of course, the story is simply a moralistic example of personal bravery (young Wyatt's) and dogged loyalty (the greyhound is the counterpart to Henry Wyatt's cat) combining to suppress outright rebellion (the lion). But the example is embedded in its use at court. It comes to us through its rehearsal in the king's own mouth, and in this rehearsal Wyatt the lion tamer is blurred with the rebellious lion that he slays, for Wyatt too seems to be a whelp (a "free and daring spirit"), whose native energies were heated to the point where the king must find some way of containing them. How better than by alluding to this story of childish bravery and rashness? When the king rehearses the allusion, it provides a way of mitigating Wyatt's recklessness, perhaps even his disregard for the king's express wishes, as a kind of boyish zeal that sometimes overran good judgment but that was basically well motivated (the lion was a "rebel"—or was Wyatt the rebel?—lions, after all, are kings).

In any case, father and son are surely cast in these stories as two different kinds of cats, and the contrast between the tales brings out the importance of generational paradigms for imagining lives historically. These are stories about sons and fathers, fathers and sons, and I foreground the complexity of this relationship because its ideological influence is invasive. The Tudor family focused intently on paternal and filial status. The notorious efforts of Henry VIII to father a son provide but the most exalted example of how Tudor families wanted sons beyond hope and reason. The eldest son is the site of privilege and anxiety, of course, in most patrilinear societies, especially under such strict primogeniture and entailment as was found in England. But in times when social and ideological change is perceived as rapid (whether or not it is), the "stabilizing" positions of fathers and sons are increasingly anxious. Fathers and mothers wanted sons desperately as dynastic guarantors of position, and they raised them not simply as chips off the old block but as opportunistic offspring who could capitalize on their family's gains and retain them under changing conditions. It is thus not surprising that these objects of uncontrolled patriarchal desire were born to be judged either brilliant successes or dismal failures, and bound to be cast as signally dutiful or egregiously rebellious. Henry VIII, for example, was praised by Thomas More in his coronation verses for putting behind him the parsimonious bookkeeping of his father in favor of a princely largesse. More's notoriously harsh words for Henry VII are uncharacteristic of a man who placed so much stress on filial piety—witness the prominence of John More in the family portrait and in More's letters. And More's judgment can indeed be construed as a conservative call for a return to an older aristocracy, an endorsement of the ways Henry VIII aligned himself with the noble magnates his father had so mistrusted, but whose habitual magnificence he had so much instilled as an aspiration in his son.

The Wyatt family stories suggest a similar paradigm, moving from the conservative catlike courtly circumspection of Henry Wyatt (a successful royal bookkeeper who built up his family fortunes by keeping the royal bureaucracy running smoothly) to the wild license enjoyed by his eldest son (who was imprisoned by his own king three times and who spent most of his adult life in desperate need of cash). There is some merit to this mythology of Thomas Wyatt as a prodigal son. But there are further implications to explore. What conditions could generate such a family mythology? What functions did it fulfill? Henry Wyatt served as one of the political "fathers" of the young Henry VIII when he ascended to the throne in 1509. He retained his offices as keeper of the jewels, keeper of the exchange, esquire of the body, and member of the council; he was knighted in the order of the Bath as part of the coronation festivities.[19] And with other advisors of his own age—men who had reached their prime in Henry VII's old age—Henry Wyatt provided the young king with well-founded advice and careful, experienced administration. He also managed to survive the purge of the administration that resulted from Henry's realignment with the nobility; indeed, he received lands seized from the notorious Empson in 1510. Thomas Wyatt, on the other hand, entered the service of an aging Henry VIII as one of the young men whose duty was in part to keep their sovereign young through the programmed recklessness of aristocratic display. Henry Wyatt's domestic career was in some senses socially and politically "radical," and his son's excessive postures were perhaps "conservative"; the same might be said of their royal masters, for Henry VIII became the refulgent renaissance prince that his father had scripted him to be—and more. The operation of patriarchy, then, as it moves between generations, is pathological. Self-conscious emulation of the father and self-proclaimed rebellion against him often belie their own terms and signal the distinct complications that ensue as patriarchal ideology plays itself out under constantly shifting historical circumstances.

The straining of generations was deeply and complexly inscribed in Wyatt's practical consciousness. The strain was one of the elements of his life that Wyatt attempted consciously to work out: it is outlined with wrenching gravity in two letters to his son that circulated widely in manuscript—someone, for example, devoutly copied them into the Egerton manuscript before it began to be used for scrap paper. They quickly became classics—Roger Ascham quotes from them—of that highly stylized genre of atavistic fatherly exhortation that survived until the triumph of bourgeois patriarchy in the eighteenth century. On the eve of his departure for a diplomatic mission to the court of Charles V in 1536, Wyatt commends his son to the example of his grandfather:

In as mitch as now ye ar come to sume yeres of vnderstanding, and that you should gather within your self sume frame of honestye, I thought that I should not lese my labour holy if now I did something advertise you to take the suer fondations and stablisht opinions, that leadeth to honestye. And here I call not honestye that men comenly cal honestye, as reputation for riches, for authoritie, or some like thing, but that honestye that I dare well say your Grandfather (whos soule god pardon) had rather left to me than all the lands he did leaue me—that was wisdome, gentlnes, sobrenes, disire to do good, frendlines to get the love of manye, and troughth above the rest.[20]

After Henry Wyatt's death, Thomas Wyatt succeeded to lands accrued in his father's lifetime of careful service: the Wyatts' principal estate, Allington Castle in Kent, purchased in 1492 and augmented by subsequent grants, as well as extensive properties in Yorkshire, Middlesex, Northhamptonshire, Surrey, and Berkshire.[21] As a man of property, he had come into his "own." Thomas Wyatt's son, also a Thomas—his expectations now clear—had been promptly married off to Jane Hawte, the daughter of a Kent neighbor, Sir William Hawte, with whom the newly married couple were now staying during Wyatt's anticipated absence. Wyatt himself had been joined by his father to the offspring of another local family—Elizabeth Brooke, daughter of Lord Cobham—some sixteen years earlier.[22] The lands upon which the fortune of Thomas Wyatt and his son depended were the rewards of the politic behavior Wyatt so commended in his father. Indeed, both Thomas Wyatt the father and Thomas Wyatt the son are distinctly heirs rather than founders of the family fortune. But heirs are also fathers, and the responsibility and the opportunity for the ambitious and cautious policy that would keep and maintain the family interests now rested with Thomas Wyatt the elder. And he is uncomfortable in his role as the fatherly figure of authority, as well he might be. For Wyatt wrote this letter from a moment of repose after crisis, and his anxiety is palpable even through the stoic calm of his pose as patriarch. Sir Henry Wyatt had died but half a year earlier on 10 November 1536, [23] just months after he had wisely helped to extricate his son from the most dangerous political scrape of his life: his imprisonment with the other suspected lovers following the fall of Anne Boleyn in May.

In writing to his own son Thomas, then, about the values that make a man, Wyatt projects onto Sir Henry the patriarchal stability he cannot sustain on his own:

And consider wel your good grandfathir what things ther wer in him, and his end; and they that knew him notid him thus: first and chiefly to haue a great reuerens of god and good opinion of godly things, next that ther was no man more piteful, no man more trew of his word, no man faster to his frend, no man diligenter nor more circumspect, which thing both the kings his masters notid in him greatly. . . . This preseruid him in prison from the handes of the tirant that could find in his hart to see him rakkid, from two yeres and more prisonment in Scotland, in Irons and Stoks, from the danger of sodeyn changes and commotions diuers, till that welbelouid of many, hatid of none, in his fair age and good reputation godly and Christenly he went to him that louid him for that he always had him in reuerens. And of myself I may be a nere example unto you of my foly and unthriftnes that hath as I wel deseruid broght me into a thousand dangers and hazardes, enmyties, hatrids, prisonments, despits, and indignations: but that god hath of his goodness chastized me and not cast me cleane out of his fauour, which thing I can impute to no thing but to the goodness of my good fathir that I dare wel say purchasid with continual request of god his grase towards me more than I regardid or considred myself, and a litel part to the smal fear that I had of god in the most of my rage and the litel delite that I had in mischiefe.[24]

Henry Wyatt's imprisonment some fifty years earlier is here invoked to cancel the almost palpable recent memory of Thomas Wyatt's own days in the Tower, here characterized as occasioned by youthful folly. But the "foly and unthriftnes" Wyatt writes of had come very close to costing him his life.

And Thomas Wyatt had in part survived because he was his father's son, following the role of son scripted for him. Wyatt had, at the age of thirty-two, freshly knighted, the father of a son himself now of age, played the role of a child submitting to correction at the hands of a series of protective fathers, from Henry Wyatt himself to Thomas Cromwell, the Wyatt family's close ally, to the king. According to the family chronicle, Henry Wyatt had been awakened in the middle of the night with a letter from Cromwell revealing that his son had been imprisoned. Having read the letter, he proclaimed, " 'If he be a true man, as I trust he is, his truth will him deliver; it is no guile,' and with this word fell asleep again very soundly until his accustomed hour, and then with all diligence, he did that by letter to the court he thought best, and which he found sufficient in the end."[25] The traces of Henry Wyatt's "diligent" correspondence with the court survive. He wrote in a reply to Cromwell after learning that his son would be released:

I have Received your leteres this xth daie of May to my grete comforte. And most humbly I thank your Maistershipp ffor the paine that ye have take [taken] to write vnto me the confortable Articles of your lettre aswell toching my son Thomas as to me. Which lettres and paine that ye have takin I nor my said son ought never to forget. Hit maie please god that wee maie deserue yt with our service. And when so euer hit shalbe the Kinges pleasure with your help to delyuer hym, that ye well shewe hym that this ponishement that he hath ffor this matter ys more ffor the displeasure that he hath done to god otherweise—Wherin I besech you to aduertice hym to fly vice and serue god better then he hath done.[26]

Henry Wyatt's language here, like the language of his letter to his son, employs the formulas of conventional piety to divert attention from actions against king and state to matters of moral failing—and thus of moral correction. Wyatt musters his authority as a father to present his son to the authority of the king in the role of a stubborn and foolish child. And he takes care to demonstrate in a later letter that he had subjected his son to a full-scale dressing down, father to son:

After I had consydered to my grete comfort with my self the kinges grete goodnes toward my son with his so ffavorable warnynges to adres hum better then his wit can consyder, I strait callyd vnto me my saide son, and as I have done oft not only commandyd hym his obediens in all pointes to the kinges pleasure, but also the leving of such slaunderus ffacon, as hath engendred vnto hym both the displeasure of god and of his maister, and as I suppose I ffownde hit not nowe to do in hym, but alredy done.

He beseeches Cromwell to stand for him as a fatherly surrogate: "And ffurther, on my blessing I have chargid hym not only to ffolowe your commaundementes ffrom tyme to tyme, but also in euery point to take and repute you as me, and if whilist he livith he have not this ffor sure printyd in his hart that I refuse hym to be my son. I besech you to contynewe vnto hym as ye have bene. And I mysknowe hym not to much, ye shall not think [yourself] evill emploide."[27] It is in precisely these terms that Thomas Wyatt nine months later commends surrogates to his son: "Think and ymagine alwais that you are in presens of some honist man that you know, as Sir Jhon Russel, your father-in law, your vnkle, parson, or some other such." And Wyatt too would flirt with a symbolic disinheritance: "I would fayne se that my lettres myght worke to frame you honist: And think that without that I esteme nothing of you, no not that you are my sone."[28]

The discourse of patriarchy then is strained and overloaded. It must bear the burden for many different kinds of power relations. It works as a way of guaranteeing continuity: in keeping his son as a child, at least in the polite language of courtly politics, Henry Wyatt is able to provide him with the benefits of a lifelong career of political favor. Then too from the point of view of a proud and worried father, the language of patriarchy "naturalizes" patronage—Cromwell is simply functioning *in loco parentis*. In other ways, it keeps sons from growing up, locking them into a prolonged and programmed adolescence, rebellious even in obedience. And it creates, just beneath the surface of father worship, the identification of the father—or the king—with the arbitrary tyrant. For is not this the other way of reading Thomas Wyatt's uneasy shift from his father's loyal imprisonment to his own scapegrace days in the Tower? Did Thomas Wyatt, too, despite the literal tenor of his words, suggest that he had submitted to a tyrant?

In any case, Henry Wyatt's strategy worked. The king liked both the Wyatts, and Cromwell and the Wyatts were tied together by faction and patronage. Thomas Wyatt's visit to his father when he was "called unto him" was doubtless imposed by the king (through Cromwell) as a mild condition of his release. And there were various strategies considered by all parties to find Wyatt a secure position or, temporarily at least, to keep him safely out of the way. There seems to have been some attempt to send him back to Calais where he had served briefly as high marshall in 1529.[29] And Henry Wyatt continued to urge that since he himself was too feeble, his son should take his place in duty and attendance upon the king.[30] Wyatt was officially given some of his father's old offices, as sheriff of Kent and co-steward of Connisborough Castle.[31] And, granted license to raise troops, he was dispatched to the north to help in the campaign against the rebellious Pilgrimage of Grace, a perfect occasion for a young man to let off his unruly spirits and to demonstrate his abiding loyalty to his royal father. Confirming the continued favor of the Wyatt family, Henry VIII himself stopped at

Allington Castle on 31 July 1536 to visit his old servant Henry Wyatt one last time.[32] Father knew best.

But now Thomas Wyatt was on his own, a man unpersuasively writing himself from a spoiled son into a father by addressing a paternalistic letter to his son. Wyatt's anxieties about his role extend even to his patriarchal abilities in the marriage bed, for he had repudiated his wife for adultery shortly after his son was born, and, just before his departure for France, his brother-in-law and others had begged Wyatt in vain to "grant her some honest living."[33] Thomas Wyatt's fatherly advice to his newly married son about the responsibilities of a husband betrays more than a touch of defensiveness:

Loue wel and agre with your wife, for where is noyse and debate in the hous, ther is unquiet dwelling. And mitch more wher it is in one bed. Frame wel your self to loue, and rule wel and honestly your wife as your felow, and she shal loue and reuerens you as her hed. Such as you are unto her such shal she be unto you. Obey and reuerens your father-in-law as you wold me; and remember that long life foloweth them that reuerens theyr fathirs and eldirs. And the blissing of god for good agrement between the wife and husband is fruyt of many children, which I for the like thinge doe lack, and the faulte is both in your mother and me, but chieflie in her.[34]

Wyatt had a difficult time wearing the mask of the patriarch; he is not confident that he has been an adequate "head" of his marriage, but he will persevere in the role. So that should his son fail to attain the "honesty" that these fatherly letters were to frame in him, "the fault shall not be in me. I shal do the part of a father."[35]

Household Economies

In reading these stories of fathers and sons, one quickly becomes aware of the overlapping households of Tudor society. Wyatt's immediate "family" is implicated in the complex structures of court, and Thomas Wyatt was very much a child of the king's household. The record of Thomas Wyatt's career in the household begins with his serving as sewer for Princess Mary's baptism in 1516; the record continues with minor errands performed through his father's offices, delivering monies, for example, from court to St. Mary's Abbey in Yorkshire in 1524.[36] In December 1527 he prepared a translation of Plutarch's *Quiet of Mind* for Queen Catherine as a New Year's gift, a work published by Pynson the following year. Such records are sketchy, of course. One wonders, for example, what Thomas Wyatt was doing in Blofflensing, Cornwall, where he was robbed in February 1533. More important, one wonders why there is no surviving record of a university degree or of a collegiate affiliation for Wyatt. He is said by his elegist John Leland to have studied at Cambridge and there is no reason to doubt the statement—it is part of the semiofficial memorial volume that issued from the royal printer after Wyatt's death.[37] A short spell at Cambridge (without taking a degree) would in no way be out of the ordinary for the son of Henry Wyatt, who could clearly see that the writing on the wall in the king's household was written in humanist italics.

But despite time spent at Cambridge or possibly elsewhere in service at a large household, Wyatt was probably living with the court through most of his adolescence and may well have done so intermittently long before. Henry Wyatt's duties as master of the jewels and plate involved constant attendance upon the king. The public record is full of page after page of Henry Wyatt's inventories of the king's belongings, from the finest jewelled regalia to the last gilt spoon. The post was not merely a matter of housekeeping. Indeed, the jewel house and the mint go together, for both were in effect "banks" where royal funds could be kept (and laundered). For the eight odd years that he served as treasurer of the chamber, 1519–27, he was in charge of one of the most important working branches of the royal fisc, for it was through this office of the king's chamber as well as through the Exchequer, the official treasury of England, and, increasingly, the king's privy chamber, that the king's income and expenses were routinely routed.

Henry Wyatt's duties as treasurer were performed in part at least out of his own "town" household, in Westminster or London, for even so central an administrator as the treasurer of the chamber did not serve in the manner of a modern bureaucrat, working out of a public office, but as a "private contractor" who provided services to the crown. Although the accounting system was sophisticated and the structure of finance carefully delineated (if complex), "the intimacy and personal—even casual—nature of the entire operation is readily apparent. The staff enjoyed social relationships both among themselves and with their clients. The focal point of the enterprise was the treasurer's private residence, and on occasion transactions could be conducted in the houses of clients."[38] In 1486, the year he was named clerk of the jewels, Henry Wyatt was granted a "messuage," a dwelling house and adjacent property, on Watling Street, in the parish of Allhallows, London.[39] As a court officer Henry Wyatt long had the privilege of daily livery at court, and since at least 1522 he had lived in apartments at Blackfriars.[40]

Allington Castle in Kent was the holding place for his family's wealth and a convenient point of departure for a courtly family "business" that was thus based largely in Westminster. Kent was not far from London by land—and it was rich and varied land at that, suitable even for delicate fruits. It sustained a thriving cloth industry and in the weald of Kent supported considerable mining, an industry in which the Wyatts had some financial interest. It was also a quick journey to London by water; the Thames forms the northern boundary of Kent, and Allington Castle, just miles from the confluence of the river Leas and the Medway and thence to the Thames, provided a direct and rapid route to court. Like Penshurst Place (its close neighbor), Allington was the perfect country home for an active courtier. And the royal household of Henry VIII depended upon Wyatt's establishment in Kent, just as it depended upon the households of the many local gentlemen—perhaps some two thousand out of a population of 2,500,000 in Henrician England—whom Thomas Elyot called the "governors" of England. These houses, spread across the shires of England, were local centers of administration. Gentry households carried out the will of the king in his land, administering the law as justices of the peace for their counties, raising arms when needed, proclaiming the king's will and enforcing it with personal influence and, when necessary, with force. These governors, in turn, could expect some influence through attendance at court or through access to someone there. And the Wyatts of Allington along with the other powerful gentry families of the rich southeast pocket of England constituted an especially powerful political force, for they combined strength "at home" (where they by far outnumbered the local peers) with strength at court (where they could also outmaneuver the titled nobility).

Even in the country at Allington, then, Thomas Wyatt was never far from the courtly source of his family's wealth and power. Thomas Wyatt himself appears to have been named as esquire of the royal body by 1524, one of the public functionaries who represented the king when visitors were received in the presence chamber. Later that year, on 21 October, Wyatt was named to his father's old position as clerk of the king's jewels (a place he would retain at least nominally until 1530),[41] and, in the 1524–25 Christmas revels, Wyatt appears to have been well enough established in the royal household to play a prominent role in the elaborate mock battle and tournament staged at Greenwich, described at length in Hall's *Chronicle*. In September 1529 he was named high marshal of Calais, where he served until November 1530.[42] In 1532, he served as justice of the peace in Essex.[43] In June 1533 he stood for his father as chief ewerer [basin bearer] at the coronation of Queen Anne.[44] In May 1534 while in attendance at court he fell into one of those escapades of aristocratic bravado that slip carelessly into violence. "On Wednesday there was a great affray between Mr. Wyatte and the serjeants of London, in which one of the serjeants was slain. For this Mr. Wyatt is committed to the Fleet."[45] Privilege protected him from prosecution beyond the mere show of justice. He may have been sent home to Allington briefly to cool off—just one month later he was licensed to have twenty men in his livery and to raise troops in Kent. In 1535 he was named (over Cromwell's nephew Richard and the abbess's own candidate) high steward of the Abbey of West Malling. He was also granted a leasehold on the substantial property of Aryngden Park, Yorkshire.[46] In March 1535 (on Easter day), he was knighted.[47]

Reading Thomas Wyatt's career, then, requires an appreciation for the work of the royal court, for these scattered references to Wyatt's official appointments outline a career far more high-powered than menial terms like "chief sewer" might at first suggest. Indeed, even Wyatt's status as a "common" gentleman is misleading. It is important to understand the terms of the court, especially in relation to the Tudor constitution as a whole. For the Council, not the court, was the nominal administrative body of the government; the most important peers and the traditional heads of departments were named to it; it was dominated by the Exchequer, the official financial office, presided over by the lord treasurer of England, and the Chancery, presided over by the lord chancellor, the nominal head of legal administration. Both these departments had facilities close to the law courts and the seat of government in Westminster. But the two other offices of the Council, Privy Seal and Signet, (headed by the Lord Privy Seal and the Secretary) were, like the Chancery (the home of the Great Seal), overlapping secretariats, responsible for transmitting the king's instructions, and they usually followed the king. The difference is important. For the Council, which generally met in Westminster, was not an independent, fully coordinated executive body; it depended upon the will of the king, and the king lived in his own large and complex household. This fluid court thus could at times provide a "cabinet" for personal government that effectively rivalled, sometimes overlapped, and sometimes displaced the Council in the continuing circulation of power.

The "court" in the first place is simply a name for the king's household; it is personal rather than constitutional. It included anyone who happened to be in attendance, and it went wherever the king went—en masse to one of the many royal residences or even in greatly reduced numbers on a hunting expedition to the small country estates of one of his intimates. Wherever it was, the court was a "liberty," exempt from the jurisdiction of local law. The composition of the court shifted continually. Each successive queen in Henry's fickle menage, for example, brought with her a separate household within the court (and thus provided the court with its only regular female population). Court could swell and shrink with the arrival of the households of visitors. And household offices had a way of shifting around. The master of the

horse for Henry VIII—his close friend Sir Antony Browne—was not even officially in the household, but he regularly kept his own table at court.[48]
Henry Wyatt's position as master of the jewel house is likewise officially outside of court in terms of budget, but very much involved in its daily life and
important enough for Thomas Cromwell to want it for himself when Henry
Wyatt gave it up in 1531. In this sense the court is an amorphous organism,
as David Loades has suggested, "always threatening to get out of control" and
resisting "the succession of ordinances and household books which were issued between 1445 and 1604" in a "constant struggle to impose order, definition, and above all economy."

In theory, however, the "court" was organized into three major departments. The easiest way to think of these three departments of court, as David
Starkey has recently suggested,[49] is to think of the living arrangements of a
Tudor king or lord. Business was conducted in a great hall; to one end of that
hall lay the kitchen and workshops that regulated household production; to
the other end lay the area where the lord received his clients and behind that,
in apartments that grew larger and more complex in the Tudor period, lay the
private living quarters of the lord and his principal attendants. The court in
turn had three principal divisions: the "hall" or "household" (thus a term for
the court as a whole and the "downstairs" of the court), which administered
the working operations of daily life and was controlled by the lord steward;
the chamber, where the king dined and received guests with all the rich
accoutrements of royal service and display, controlled by the lord chamber-
lain; and the privy or secret chamber, in charge of the groom of the stool,
where close personal servants in constant attendance upon the king catered to
the care and feeding of their monarch, from evacuation upon the close stool
to the choice of clothes from the closet and a quick game of dice or cards.

Throughout the reign of Henry VIII, he and his ministers struggled over
the administration of the household. The underlying issue, of course, was not
efficiency in the quotidian management of household affairs but the exercise
of political power. Henry VIII and Wolsey shifted around one another, for example, by instituting the office of "gentlemen of the privy chamber" in 1518
and 1519, thus giving an institutional place to the king's personal favorites
(but agreeing to place some of Wolsey's men in positions of control). Wolsey
attempted to curb the power of these minions further with household reform,
the famous Eltham ordinances of 1526, and Cromwell too played a hand in
attempts to control this unruly organism. But the shapelessness of court was
functional, for it permitted the competing interests of the court—family,
friendship, ideology, faction, patronage—to operate in different channels
with and against one another. Its fluidity gave different interests access to the

king; and it allowed the king, on the other hand, to surround himself, when he so wished, with people who agreed with him, or at least whom he found agreeable. The multiple accounting system that men like Henry Wyatt administered left a lot of room for political maneuvering; it suggests how personal the conduct of business could be, for with multiple avenues of access to the royal purse both the king and his ministers could find a multitude of ways—through personal connections—to accomplish ends that might have been stopped by a less fluid system. The different departments of the administration could be played off against one another. Henry Wyatt's appointment as treasurer, for example, was surely part of Wolsey's attempt to stem the influence of the king's intimates in the privy chamber—yet Henry VIII as well as Wolsey "liked" Henry Wyatt. And because the administration was organized personally, the functions of different offices could be combined; Henry Wyatt's accounts for the jewel house, for example, might be merged with other accounts for which he was responsible as treasurer. Thus, as J. D. Alsop has argued, "unofficial relationships did as much as central control by the monarch and Council to bring cohesion to what was, particularly from the 1530s onwards, a disparate structure."[50]

The accounts of treasurers of the chamber like Henry Wyatt are bewildering records of the subtle and twisting paths which influence could work in the unruly circulation of power within the court. The treasury of the chamber was until the 1530s the "most important revenue department in the kingdom,"[51] and in Wyatt's administration the household wages[52] and the most important matters of public expenditure passed through his hands. But there seems to have been a double system of accounting even within the chamber as Henry moved money for the payment of major public expenses from the treasury account to the account of the privy purse, sums which the wary Wolsey insisted upon accounting for.[53] It is hardly surprising, then, that in Wyatt's accounts, as in those of his predecessors, the "prevailing impression is one of informality."[54] Money moves here in mysterious ways, through third parties, and for unknown reasons.

This fluid circulation of interests around the king also provided a subtle vehicle for the operation of personal ambition; the traditional departments of government, the departments of the court, the changing whims of king, queen, and minister—all these created a mazed path of preferment that was motivated by the interaction of men perceived not simply by status, rank, or office, but as "selves" or "personalities." As masters, as servants, as social equals, in particular as members of adjacent ranks, the men of the early Tudor court were hypersensitive and suspicious about how they were perceived by one another because personal matters—desires, loyalties, fancies, hatreds—were what made power work. This is what Thomas Wyatt would call the "slipper toppe of worldes estate," and its very slipperiness was simultaneously an advantage and a danger to the young man on the rise. Advancement could be personal; there was no orderly progression through the bureaucratic ranks. Nor was there a predictable fall from grace; the way down was always sudden and precipitous. Success depended upon the evaluations and judgments of important people.

Wyatt's first official positions at court, then, as clerk of the jewels, as soldier, as high marshall of Calais, are not in themselves indicative of his skills as a courtier—they could have fallen in the way of any favorite son towards whom a powerful figure such as Cromwell or even Henry Wyatt himself chose to direct patronage. But Thomas Wyatt advanced his career at court in ways his father could not have done. Wyatt quickly became known for possessing a certain rhetorical power and personal charm. He was a man men talked about; he was "witty"; he could persuade others with his own words and analyze the motives of theirs; and this skill in persuasion and in the psychology of courtly discourse won him diplomatic appointments that thrust him into the center of Henry's dynastic international politics as the king's personal representative abroad. Wyatt's grandson tells a story, learned from his father, of how Wyatt won one such diplomatic appointment, accompanying Sir John Russell to the papal court in 1527. Sailing down the Thames about to embark, Sir John is supposed to have encountered Wyatt, "and after salutations was demanded of him whither he went, and had answer 'To Italy, sent by the King.' 'And I,' said Sir Thomas, 'will, if you please, ask leave, get money, and go with you.' 'No man more welcome,' answered the ambassador. So this accordingly done they passed in post together."[55]

Such is the easy wit that makes promoting the interests of friends a pleasure among gentlemen who understand one another. The quick word in the right place at the right time is just what is required, as well as a sharp eye and an ear keenly attuned to the diffuse play of courtly rhetoric—speeches, jests, shouts, and laughter that animated the daily routine of the household from the morning levee to cards after supper. As Sir Thomas Cheney wrote to Wolsey in sending Wyatt back with a message from his first mission (to France in 1526), Wyatt will provide excellent intelligence about the courtly politics of Francis I's household, for he has "as much wit to mark and remember everything he seeth as any young man hath in England."[56]

This skill won Wyatt five major diplomatic appointments. The first mission to Francis I in 1526 was a complicated stalling maneuver; Wyatt was to accompany Cheney, a Kentish neighbor, to France, offering congratulations to Francis on his return to France after his capture at the disastrous battle of

Pavia and vying for position as France, Florence, Venice, Milan, and the pope entered the holy league of Cognac in a vain attempt to resist Charles V's hold on Italy. A second embassy to the papacy and Venice in 1527 (accompanying Sir John Russell, another neighbor in the small world of suburban Kent) brought Wyatt to Italy in the midst of the invasion of Charles V; Wyatt left Rome days before it was sacked in a brutal imperial march that shocked and fascinated Christian Europe. From 1537 to 1539 and again from 1539 to 1540 Wyatt followed the imperial court, in Spain as well as in France and the Low Countries, charged with the impossible task of negotiating Henry VIII's changing marital status with Charles V (his former brother-in-law) and maintaining a strong strategic position for England as Francis I and Charles V negotiated a new alliance.

Writing Home

A diplomat in the personal polity of the renaissance court was above all a personal spokesman. He was sent literally to speak with a king as the rhetorical surrogate of a king. When Cromwell gave Wyatt his instructions sending him to the emperor's court in 1537, he was explicit about just what kind of rhetorical agency was demanded:

Your parte shalbe nowe like a good Oratour, bothe to set furthe the princely nature and inclynacion of his highnes with all dexteritie, and soo to obseruve Themperours answers to the said Ouerture and to the rest of the points in the same letteres expressed, as you may therby fishe out the botom of his stomake, and aduertise his Maieste howe he standethe disposed towardes him, and to the contynuance of thamytie betweene them. . . . Contynue vigilant nowe in thenserching out of thinges mete to be knowen. . . . Gentle Maister Wiat nowe use all your wisedom.[57]

Orator is the normal term in sixteenth-century Latin usage for diplomat. An orator is thus literally spokesman for his sovereign; his speech is expected to set forth "his highnes," to project in words the magnificence of the monarch. His powers of observation, on the other hand, are to be devoted to stripping off the emperor's magnificence to the "botom of his stomake." The position of the orator thus by definition traces out the contradictions in the ideology of royal power. An orator has to read and speak between the lines of the script written to make royal power appear unquestionable; he must give credit to absolutism in his every word and gesture, honoring the sovereign body politic of the king; but he must also expose the fragile personal body of the man who wears the crown. He must represent his English prince, and he must insinuate his personal presence into the intimate operations of another foreign court. He must be likable, but he cannot follow his own likes or dislikes. He must speak spontaneously, with all the assertive license of a court wit, but he must not depart from the letter of his monarch's written instructions. As Wyatt's instructions read for presenting Henry's greetings to Francis in May 1526, they are to be "well couched in the French tongue and not as an oration, but as a familiar, friendly, and kind message."[58] And then when the tongues of court are still, the orator must in private write down what has been said for his king to read. Diplomatic "dexteritie" must be put to work here as well, for when the orator writes back to his own sovereign, he must decide with care just what to record for the king and how, as well as who else should or should not know about it.

The letters of ambassadors, then, contain the traces of many different kinds of discourse. They are marked by the many voices they transcribe. They are scandalous examples of writing purporting to be a simple transcription of speech. Indeed, there is perhaps no better image for the unruly circulation of power at court than the exchanges of diplomatic letters, for ambassadors do not write like historians with an eye to posterity; their search for information is rapacious, invasive, and sometimes indiscriminate; they turn gossip into intelligence, and so it is: "A secretary of Grandvela told a friend of myne this other daye that ther was newes come owt of Fraunce that made the emperour so jocund that he skant colde tell on what ground he stoode," Wyatt wrote to Henry VIII from Ghent on 24 March 1540.[59]

I do not mean to suggest that these letters are artless. Indeed, letters from abroad by Wyatt, Wriothsley, Cecil, and other successful courtiers are perhaps among the greatest practical achievements of humanist rhetoric: in their most telling moments they become narratives in a mode of neoclassical "realism," fleshing out courtly scenes with the "personal" touches of reported dialogue and details of decor, dress, and demeanor; at times they read like scenes from book 1 of More's *Utopia* or like the classical letters or histories that provided their models. Indeed, one might argue that this kind of realism—it savors of Plutarch or of Cicero's letters to Atticus—is a key discursive means for enabling the court to be perceived as real, as a locus of power, as a place where personal matters carried public weight. And it is here in the eddying circulation of letters from parts of Europe distant to one another and from distant parts within the realm itself that one can find an image of the partiality, embarrassment, embeddedness, and scandal of courtly politics.

No letters could be sent person-to-person. The letters were written by the orator, often transcribed by a secretary so that the correspondent could keep his "original." They were carried by couriers posting horse after horse in a rapid journey home and back at great expense—Wyatt's courier in Spain, Nicholas de la Pelle, received £30 in payment, a living allowance of £54, and £250 for post horses for a few months service.[60] And the letters often passed through many hands. Wyatt, for example, often posted letters through the services of a passing friend; sometimes he sent them to Lord Lisle at Calais, who sent them across the Channel on one of his regular relays. Letters were sometimes sent in cypher, of course, the letter and the cypher being posted back by two separate couriers to maintain secrecy. But even the open letters must in a sense be decoded by being reinserted into the overlapping correspondences of which they are a part. Wyatt writes to Henry to tell him what he has said and done as Henry's surrogate; and then he writes to Cromwell to tell him the same thing, but slightly differently. And another ambassador writes to Cromwell or to the king to tell him what Wyatt said. And the emperor or the king sends letters to his ambassador in England reporting the same news. And someone reads the letters along the way, and passes the information on into yet another cycle of circulation. Orators are dispatched with letters to deliver to the foreign prince in what the English called "doubles," one copy for the orator, one for presentation; the cypher copy is also called a "double." And always the language passes through translations: Spanish to English; English to Spanish; French to English; Latin everywhere. Orators, then, are complex and redoubling "spokesmen," as their written "correspondence" demonstrates, for their discourse is fractured by the heterogeneous work it performs; orators "speak" for their kings, but at the same time they speak for themselves, for their patrons, for their court faction, for their theological interests; they speak foreign voices that they do not understand; and they speak to different people differently.

The vaunting majesty of the renaissance court with its pageants and entries is transparent to the accomplished orator, although he knows how to use its ceremonies. Wyatt commented, for example, on the ceremony accompanying Charles's alliance with Francis at Fontainebleau as he wrote from Paris on Christmas Day 1539: "But we se not for all thes entrys, for all this joyning of armes, knyttyng of crowns, and such cerymonys, that thei shold determin to part the world bytwene them."[61] And when the magnificence no longer renders the court opaquely homogeneous, the courtly polity becomes the site for the operation of differences. As Wyatt wrote to Cromwell of the duke of Cleves's claim to Gelderland as a dowry for marrying the duchess of Milan (Henry VIII had tried for the duchess, just as he was currently being nudged into marriage to Anne of Cleves), "But I dowt nothing now so much as that he be begilid with practicis and that he makyth not his surest fondation where he shold. . . . These men ar not drawen by curtesi, frendshipp or equite, but by interest."[62]

Wyatt's goal as an ambassador, then, as he expresses it again and again in his letters, was to penetrate into that world of personal interest, into the inner workings of the court, into the king's intimacy, into his private thoughts, into his stomach. The image repeated throughout Wyatt's letters and those of other brilliant diplomatic correspondents is one of withdrawal: from public audience into an inner space; into the privy chamber; into the private recesses of a window, a movement often accompanied by an act of uncovering or moving forward. Wyatt and Cheney, for example, are reported to have visited the French court on Whitsun 1526, after Francis I had dined in his privy chamber "secretly bycause he had taken his ryghtys. And at our first entering he was leaning out at a window talking with the Great Master, who is most in favor of any man," when the king turns to them and "removes his bonnet." In 1539 Wyatt reports to Henry about his reception by Charles V: "and the next morning abowt ix of the clok I had accesse vnto hym where he receyvid me (the conestable being in the chamber) gentilly with his hatt in his hand."[63]

At times access was not so easy to come by, for it was not directly from the king or emperor but through his intermediaries, like the constable of France, who "now hath the stroke alone,"[64] or Charles's powerful minister Grandevela:

The next day affter the entry off th' emperour in this towne both my Lord of London and I sent to the conestable for our audience; that sent vs rownd word that there was no tyme for that day. The next day in the morning . . . we went our selffes to his chamber dore; but he eskapid vs by a bake dore. Never the lesse affter the kynges masse we spake with hym and he forthwith spake with the kyng and came agayne, [and] apoynted vs our audience affter the kynges dyner, offerynge vs to dyne with hym. Wich bycawse we were far off logid and farr a sonder, we refusid not. And for bycawse that peradventure the sayd conestable myght have taken some fansy to have hindered the matter if we shold have made this ouerture to the kyng withowt participating the thing afore with hym, we semyng to fownd ourselffes apon the gret confidence that we knew your maiestie had in hym in aduancing your affaires, told hym that we wold participate.[65]

But such "access" even when it is granted more easily is never complete and again and again in the letters the sense of personal presence so warmly evoked by humanist realism recedes into uncertainty: "I wot nott, by our lord, what I may wryte vnto your maiestie off eny certaintye, ffor I see litill aparence wich way I may come to knollege—all that I may do is conjecture. Here is comen few or none off my familiars."[66] And the uncertainty shades off into insecurity, for the play of interests in courtly politics never stops, and Wyatt, as a blind player in a court three weeks away by letter, lets slip his mask of confidence: "My coniectures myght be more certaine if it plesid your highnes that I myght be so much trustid as to have some aduertisement of your other intelligences and other mens coniectures."[67]

All around the court swirls an eddy of words. Wyatt tries to interpret it; at times he will advise Henry to try to manipulate it, suggesting, for example, that frequent formal letters (with no pressing content) would give Wyatt an excuse to press his case in audience or that some propaganda in German would advance his majesty's interests.[68] But the diffuse circuits of power defy efforts to secure them. As Charles V told Wyatt when he complained that Spanish preachers were inciting the people against England and its lustful king, "I woll tel yow, Monsieur l'embassadeur . . . kynges be not kinges of tonges, and if men gyve cause to be spoken off, thei woll be spoken off: there is no remedy."[69]

In years of attendance at the court of Charles V, Wyatt became something of an old Spanish hand, and his mature style as an ambassador is visible especially in his letters of 1537–41. He was adept at projecting himself into the intellectual intimacy of the emperor. At times he patiently presented stalling strategies, hoping to feel his interlocutor out and thus lead into the English position. At times he literally presented letters from the king and waited for the reply. And at times he took risks. Wyatt often took to playing the role of the Protestant bad boy, parrying with Charles about contemporary issues. He protested, for example, the treatment of English merchants by the Inquisition, commenting that these were not heretics like Anabaptists or Sacramentaries but simply differed about the authority of the bishop of Rome. Charles replied:

"The kynge is of one opinion and I am of an other; and tho, as yow say, there were communication apon this it was not agred to. I assure yow if yowr marchantes come with eny intollerances [that is, intolerable theological positions] I can not lett [stand in the way of] the Inquisition. This is a thing that towchetch our fayth." "What, Sir" quod I, "the primacy of the bishopp of Rome?" "Ye, mary," quod he, "it is playne agayne the principall. There be thinges that mak fore it that itt is, *De Jure divino*, canon and Cyvile [There are arguments for this point according to divine law, canon law, and civil law] and this is a poynt against the pryncypall." "Sir," quod I, "almost thei themsellfes [that is, the popes] durst neuer claime that *de jure divino*." "What!"

quod he, "Monsiuer l'embassadeur, shall we now come to dispute that of *tibi dabo claves?*"[70]

It is thus no surprise that Wyatt had a reputation among the Spanish as a notoriously radical ambassador. He himself was interrogated by the Inquisition, and he was thought by many to be a hothead. These were useful credentials, of course, at home or at least in his own faction at court, where Cromwell and Cranmer were slowly moving the English church towards a protestant practice. And this performance surely did gain him a certain prominence at the imperial court. But who is speaking in these reported dialogues? Wyatt the ambassador? Wyatt the loyal servant of Cromwell? Wyatt the man of deeply protestant conscience? Wyatt the show-off? Was Wyatt simply trying to bring his impossible mission to a close by demonstrating that Charles would not be moved? "I have owt of my custome holden your maiestie with long lettres," Wyatt wrote to Henry, "ffor that I saw in this accesse to th'emperour that vehemence that I have not been acustomid to se. I notyd his lowder voyce, his ernester looke, and specially his imperius fashon in his wordes, namely in the thinges of the Inquisition."[71]

It was precisely this kind of question that Wyatt's fellow ambassador, the querulous Edmund Bonner, raised about Wyatt in a long letter of complaint to Cromwell in September 1538. Bonner, who was elected bishop of London while abroad on this mission, and Simon Heynes, the dean of Exeter, had been sent to assist Wyatt in April 1538. Henry may well have been impatient with Wyatt's embassy (so was Wyatt), and it is surely no surprise that the two ambassadors, virtually set up to be rivals, did not get along. Bonner grants that Wyatt is consummately agreeable: "Wittie he is, and pleasant among companye, contented to make and kepe chere," but the problem is that this bonhomie is excessive and its motives suspicious, for to Bonner Wyatt's courtly wit is intended not to advance Henry's policies but Wyatt's own standing in the eyes of the imperial court. After enjoying a daylong feast at the emperor's lodging, Bonner claims, Wyatt went "from thence to Jonkaes, a place of nunnes, wher the fest and solempnite was kept, talking with themperour all the waye, and after such mery sorte and fashion that expostulation was turned to obliuion." His motives, to Bonner, were clear: "And surelie that is a great marke that he shoteth at, to please themperor and Grandevele, and to be noted in the emperours favour, whom he magnifieth aboue all mesure."[72] According to Bonner, Wyatt is supposed to have claimed "that he was made a God here with the king and his counsaill."[73]

Bonner is a mean man; his letter to Cromwell is divided into numbered paragraphs beginning "I mislike Mr. Wyat that. . . ." His letters patently reveal his wounded *amour propre*: he was insulted by Wyatt, who left him out of meetings and excluded him from close contacts with Grandvela and Charles. There are other more substantive charges, to be sure: that Wyatt had failed to gain favorable terms for England in the Treaty of Nice (June 1538); that Wyatt had said that unless Henry assented to Charles's notions about his next bride, he should deservedly be "cast out at the cart's tail"; that Wyatt had instructed his subordinate John Mason to enter into talks with Reginald, Cardinal Pole, upon whom rested the pope's hopes for regaining England. These charges were investigated by the king and council during Wyatt's absence, as Cromwell cautiously warned him. Mason was examined by the council, as was Elizabeth Darrell, Wyatt's mistress, with whom Wyatt had visited while in England briefly in June. The charges were not pursued at this point. They would be taken up again after Thomas Cromwell's fall in 1540, when the personal balance of power shifted and Wyatt (12 January 1541) would once again be taken to the Tower and charged with treason.

But the charges that do have some interest are perhaps the most trivial ones about Wyatt's behavior as a flamboyant courtier. Boastful speech and bitter personal rivalries had in fact foiled the repeated English efforts to eliminate Cardinal Pole. Wyatt boasts with unconcealed eagerness about some such secret plan rather unsubtly in several dispatches back to England. Sir Francis Bryan, who was in charge of recruiting the assassins, seems to have boasted of his undercover activities to members of the French court, who then tipped off Pole; Lord Lisle in Calais (where some of the action was supposed to originate) had a longstanding personal animosity against Sir Robert Wingfield, whose retainers had been given key jobs in the operation that somehow never were accomplished; Elizabeth Darrell, Wyatt's mistress, whom Wyatt and others had confided in, seems to have played a part in a chain of gossip that also eventually passed the news on to the Pole circle.[74] Pole claimed that Wyatt had declared that if Henry VIII would relieve him of his embassy, proclaim Pole a public enemy, and give him £10,000 he would wager his possessions in England that he could procure Pole's death within six months, most suitably in Rome. To Pole, these remarks seemed *temere et impie dicta a furioso juvene* [the impious and rash remarks of a wild young man], but he was still on the watch, for, indeed, Pole had been declared an enemy, Wyatt had been recalled—and no one knew where he was.[75]

Bonner, then, who would never be the winning courtier that Wyatt was (he later proved, however, to be adept at burning heretics), hits precisely upon the vital contradiction in the psychology of the successful courtier, whose self-dramatization inevitably conflicts with the master plot scripted for his sovereign lord. One detail from Bonner's charges is particularly telling. He claims that Wyatt continually harped upon his imprisonment following Queen Anne's fall in 1536:

I mislike that Mr. Wyat, in his communication touching his legation with themperour, dooth often call to his remembraunce his emprisonement in the Towere, which semeth soo to sticke in his stomacke that he can not forget it; and his manner of speking therein is after this sorte, "Goddes bludde! was not that a prety sending of me ambassadour to themperour, first to put me into the Tower, and then furthewith to send me hither? This was a waye indede to get me credite here. By godds precious bludde, I had rather the king shuld set me in Newgate [a London prison for common criminals] then soo doo."[76]

Bonner had no sense of humor, clearly. But Wyatt's reported remarks are telling, for as his letters to his son suggest, the bloody days of May in the Tower in 1536 were a strain on Wyatt's consciousness. Wyatt's poem from the Tower laments, "The bell tower showed me such sight / That in my head stickes day and night." Bonner may have had a point, for Wyatt's imprisonment in the Tower indeed seems to surface with suggestive indirection at odd moments. When Wyatt and an assistant, for example, succeeded in capturing a traitorous Englishman who had joined Charles V and Charles insisted that he be returned, Wyatt tells Henry VIII that Charles had exclaimed, "Ffor surely I aduertise you, that tho your master had me in the tower of London, I wold not consent to change myne honour and my consciens."[77] Who is speaking here, Charles, the Holy Roman Emperor, or Thomas Wyatt, former prisoner of the Tower?

The Death of Wyatt and the Name of an Author

Bonner's charges against Wyatt never came to trial in 1539—Cromwell dutifully investigated and suppressed them after learning that they were insubstantial. That these same charges were raised again in the months after Cromwell's fall testifies to the efficiency with which the law can play to the need for a scapegoat in uneasy times. There had been rampant fear in England for the past few years (throughout Wyatt's embassy) of a foreign invasion; musters had been held throughout the realm; one of the resident foreign ambassadors had commented that the English were so irritable that even asking a question made them think you were starting a quarrel. The vacuum in the paths of patronage and influence created at court by Cromwell's fall had made the anxiety even worse. Wyatt had witnessed Cromwell's execution—he wrote a poem of mourning for his patron—and had been so distraught, according to a contemporary account, that he was prevented by his tears from answering the condemned minister's request for prayers. The arrest of Wyatt in January 1541 provided the excuse for a public display of national security. The French ambassador Marillac comments, as do other foreign observers, on the novelty of the public humiliation of a gentleman being led out with his hands bound: "that last night, by order of the King two much esteemed gentlemen of the court were taken as prisoners from Hampton Court to this town, and this morning they were seen conducted with hands tied, conducted by twenty four archers to the great Tower of London . . . . One is Master Wyatt . . . though neither earl nor baron, [he] was one of the richest gentlemen in England, having as income from his patrimony six or seven thousand ducats a year."[78] Marillac may exaggerate Wyatt's annual income and power, but he does pick up the irony of Wyatt's fall from indisputable wealth. In March 1540 he had received substantial leaseholds in Kent, Surrey, and London—most notably Boxley Abbey in Kent and the priory of the Crutched Friars in the city—in exchange for surrendering some of his other Kent properties.[79] The reversal in fortune was dramatic and perhaps predictable. As Marillac comments, "Although he is more regretted than any man taken in England these three years, both by Englishmen and by foreigners, no man is bold enough to say a word for him, and by these fine laws he must be judged, without knowing why." Marillac points out that this is worse than any war the English could inflict on themselves, for after Cromwell had brought down all the greatest, "now others have arisen who will never rest till they have done as much to Cromwell's servants, and God knows whether after them others will not recommence the feat."

The Privy Council sent Sir Richard Southwell to Allington to seize all of Wyatt's household goods, to discharge his daughter-in-law and his friend Lady Poynings, both staying at Allington, and to dismiss his servants with half a year's wages and an honest lesson. Compassionately, Southwell was instructed to allow Wyatt's pregnant mistress, Elizabeth Darrell, to stay in the house, "lest that might perishe which she had conceyved."[80] Wyatt wrote a declaration of his innocence that he delivered to the Privy Council; he also prepared an oration in his defense, a brilliant example of his rhetorical training. But when things had cooled down in March, he duly "confessed" to everything that had been charged, yielded himself to the mercy of the king, and received his pardon, according to the Privy Council report, after great suit by Queen Catherine Howard. According to Chapuis, a further condition of his release was "that he should take back his wife from whom he had been separated upwards of 15 years, on pain of death if he be untrue to her henceforth."[81] He returned to royal service through the usual back door, being named captain in charge of three hundred light cavalry to protect Calais as new fortifications were prepared. By February 1542 Wyatt was close enough to royal favor—though through what route remains a mystery—to be given several offices that had belonged to Thomas Culpepper, the alleged lover of the late Queen Catherine Howard, herself now the victim of court intrigue.[82] In March he was named high steward of the manor of Maidstone in Kent,[83] and through a complicated exchange of property with the king, became the owner of a rich package of lands in Kent, Dorset, and Somerset, including substantial holdings surrounding Montague Priory.[84] There were rumors in August that Wyatt would be named captain of a galley and vice-admiral of the fleet being readied for a forthcoming war with France,[85] and in October Wyatt was sent by the king to ride post haste to Falmouth to greet his old acquaintance Monmorency de Corrierez, an envoy of Charles V, and escort him back to court at Westminster. Wyatt never reached Falmouth. A sudden and violent fever forced him to stop for rest at the house of a friend, Sir John Horsey, where he quickly succumbed—exhausted, an epitaph relates, by hard riding on frequently posted horses and by the heat of the sun. He was buried in the great collegiate church at Sherborne, possibly in the Horsey family tomb. The registry of burial states simply: "On October 11 was buried/Sir Thomas Wyatt, Councillor of the King,/A man of great worship."[86]

The death and burial of this important royal servant would probably remain unremarkable, fitting seamlessly into the daily weave of Henrician politics, were it not for the immediate and continuing reinscription of this royal orator as the author of a national secular literature. As David Starkey has commented, Wyatt's life "though dramatic, was in no way unusual. Every aspect of it could be paralleled in the biographies of a dozen or more of his contemporaries at the court of Henry VIII."[87] But there is no parallel to the ways in which contemporaries at court describe the cultural importance of his poetry and set the pattern for the reception of Wyatt in the decades that followed. Within months of Wyatt's death, two extraordinary memorial volumes were issued in print, one a collection of Latin elegies, *Naeniae in mortem Thomas Wyattis, equitis incomparabilis*, by John Leland, who served as the royal antiquary and claimed to be an old Cambridge friend of Wyatt's, and the other *An excellent Epitaffe of syr Thomas Wyatt*, by the scion of one of the most powerful dynasties of the realm, Henry Howard, earl of Surrey.

Both these productions seem to come out of the same factional milieu. Leland's volume is dedicated to Surrey, who is glowingly represented as Wyatt's literary heir. Both elegies inscribe Wyatt's life within the larger economy of the court and national culture; these larger inscriptions are important to understanding how the field of human letters was being used to secure contradictory processes. Leland's verses evoke the accomplishments of a versatile and exemplary courtier whose loyal service to the king, whose eloquence, whose manly appearance, whose learning and military prowess will win him everlasting fame. Leland even provides a "prosopographia" or portrait in words so that those who have not seen Wyatt will know the "whole appearance of the man in life." Surrey's poem, an epicedium spoken as if from the foot of the grave, provides an anatomical blazon of Wyatt's parts, pathetically writing the lost Wyatt into wholeness as "a valiant corpse, where force and beauty met." Both these works, then, like so many institutions of the emerging early modern state, construct a "whole man" by inscribing a kind of totalizing significance upon the many (contradictory) aspects of his life, even literally putting together a whole body out of anatomical parts. Like other rehearsals of the "uomo universale," not only in biographical description but in conduct manuals and ethical treatises, these descriptions of Wyatt are, in part, a way of "treating the body as a memory," and entrusting "to it in abbreviated and practical, i.e., mnemonic form the fundamental principles of the arbitrary content of the culture."[88]

But within this context, both Leland and Surrey authorize another specifically literary economy. Like later literary commemorations—the verses on the death of Prince Henry, the elegies for Sidney's death, the memorial verses in Shakespeare's first folio—these elegies create a discursive space for conceptualizing the agency of letters in the ongoing production of culture. Both elegies equate poetic and national power; both stress the example Wyatt has set for literary form. In Leland's words:

> Bella suum merito jactet florentia Dantem
> Regia Petrarchae carmina Roma probet.
> His non inferior patrio sermone Viatus
> Eloquii secum qui decus omne tulit.

[Beautiful Florence boasts with merit of Dante; and regal Rome commends the songs of Petrarch. In the tongue of our fatherland Wyatt is not inferior to these, for he has won for himself the shining prize of eloquence.][89]

As others would throughout the century, Leland imagines Wyatt as one who "polishes" his crude vernacular:

> Anglica lingua fuit rudis & sine nomine rhythmus
> Nunc limam agnoscit docte Viate tuum.

[The English tongue was rude, its verse without renown; Now learned Wyatt, it may be proud to have known your file.]

> Nobilitas didicit te praeceptore Britanna
> Carmina per varios scribere posse modos.

[The British nobility have now learned, with you as a teacher, to write verses in many forms.]

Surrey's verses, which preceded Leland's by a few months, employ similar tropes of a whole man embodying a national culture:

> A head, where wisdom mysteries did frame,
> Whose hammers beat still in that lively brain
> As on a stithe, where that some work of fame
> Was daily wrought to turn to Britain's gain. . . .
>
> A hand that taught what might be said in rhyme;
> That reft Chaucer the glory of his wit;
> A mark the which, unparfited for time,
> Some might approach, but never none shall hit.
>
> A tongue that served in foreign realms his king
> Whose courteous talk to vertue did enflame
> Each noble heart; a worthy guide to bring
> Our English youth by travail unto fame.[90]

Both elegies, then, elide the personal genius or "wit" of Wyatt and the nation of Britain; his individual achievement as a master poet produces the glory of the state; in Surrey's poem Wyatt the man emerges from the catalogue of his anatomical parts as the moral voice of a nation. The name of Wyatt is thus canonized here in part as a confirmation of emerging nationalism—a phrase like "Britain's gain" even picks up on the imperial and romantic savor of the relatively new Tudor usage of "Britain," and one sees in the personal piety and moral exactingness of the Wyatt canonized here the figuring of nationalism, protestantism, and aristocracy that was so important as England grew into her role as a protestant state with the court as an ideological center. But the name of Wyatt is also canonized in part because it is seen as independent from the state, as if it had some authority or some distance that allowed for a critique of its own culture. Wyatt is inscribed in the early Tudor period then both as a national poet or courtly maker—this is the designation, of course, that sticks as Wyatt and Surrey are passed on to the Elizabethans—and also a poet of courage, conscience, even opposition. Wyatt's translations of the penitential psalms, Surrey writes, provide a place

> Where Rewlers may se in a myrrour clere
> The bitter frewte of false concupiscense,
> How Jewry bought Uryas deathe full dere.
> In Princys hartes Goddes scourge yprinted depe
> Myght them awake out of their synful slepe.[91]

Wyatt's name, however, is canonized not only in elegy, but by readers as his poems circulate at the court. Thomas Wyatt the younger inherited the Egerton manuscript when his father died;[92] he allowed Nicholas Grimald to use it to prepare an "authorized" printed edition of the penitential psalms in 1549 when other corrupt copies were apparently available. And when he was in the Tower, awaiting the inevitable sentence of death following his unsuccessful rebellion against Queen Mary, he brought the volume with him, and passed it on to a fellow prisoner, Sir John Harrington of Stepney, in whose family the volume remained for generations. Harrington copied Surrey's "The great Macedon," which I quoted from above, into the Egerton manuscript as a preface to the psalms; he also copied his own translation into the volume following Wyatt's poems. Another hand copied Wyatt's letters to his son; yet another—apparently confused by some of the layering of hands at one point—wrote "finis quod Wyatt." Someone else has occasionally written "Wyatt" in the margins. There are many more layers of hands. And the Wyatt poems circulated elsewhere as well. John Harrington, for example, copied many of the poems from Egerton MS. 2711 into a manuscript of his own, now known as the Arundel-Harrington manuscript. And in 1545 Wyatt's own close friend, George Blage, whom Leland says Wyatt honored for his sharp wit, purchased (and subsequently added to) a manuscript of poems arranged uniquely in groups by alphabetical order (according to first words) that included a few poems known to be Wyatt's. Another codex, the Devonshire manuscript, passed through many people known to Wyatt, especially two women, Mary Shelton, a member of the Howard circle, and Mary Howard, lady Fitzroy, sister of the earl of Surrey and wife of Surrey's childhood companion, the illegitimate son of Henry VIII, who Harrier speculates first purchased the volume around 1533. This is a shared, collective volume that shows poems being used by members of the court in literary recreation. In this busy manuscript, one of the hands at least takes the business of attribution seriously, assigning poems to "Wyatt" or "W," to Wyatt's brother-in-law Sir Antony Lee, to someone named Richard Hatfield, or, at times, to "somebody" and "nobody."[93] I suppose that this hand "meant" that the author was not known. But there were also times when the author could not be named. In 1557, when Richard Tottel published his miscellany, *Songs and Sonnets*, containing large selections of Wyatt's and Surrey's poems, he proclaimed that he was releasing these poems from the "gentle hoarders up" of poetry in manuscript.[94] Wyatt's name does not even appear on the title page of this volume, which advertises poems by Henry Howard, earl of Surrey, and "other." But the reason is understandable. The Howards were a prominent Catholic family, and the duke of Norfolk, Surrey's father, had just been released from nearly ten years imprisonment in the Tower under Edward VI and the Seymours, while Thomas Wyatt the younger had just been executed for high treason. Inside the volume, Wyatt is clearly identified. What matters is that a body of poetry attached to the name of Thomas Wyatt had survived, and survived as "his." Whatever coincidence of social functions led Wyatt to collect his poems as a group in the first place was also strong enough in others as these poems circulated to retain the sense that they were "Wyatt's." Poems were now being understood in relation to the name of their author.

Chapter Two

Signatures

A drawing now in the British Library shows Henry VIII dining in the privy chamber.[1] He sits alone at a long table upon a dais and under a large peaked canopy at the center of one end of the hall. The vaulting canopy and a luxuriously folded backdrop behind it display the royal badges and arms. A small group of courtiers attends him, knees slightly bent as they approach the table. The image of the king at table dominates the drawing. But it is a busy composition. In the corners of the hall other groupings are visible. In the left corner, just in front of a window, stand three gentlemen intent in conversation and turned away from the king. Beyond them appears another group whose attention is just now being drawn to the royal table. This drawing—possibly after a lost Holbein sketch—suggests the magnificent scale of public life in the royal court and the ideological centering of the king as the source of power. It also suggests the intricate and overlapping groupings and networks of people subsumed within the circuitous organization of the king's household and producing in their contradictory modes of behavior the magnificence of the Tudor monarch. Given the diffusive constitution of the Tudor court it is perhaps not surprising that in many ways the viewer's interest in the sketch draws him beyond the public presentation of the king to the private groups that the production of his massive personal presence makes intriguing and important even as its magnificence appears to obscure them.

And within the court, it is perhaps not surprising to see the public and the private increasingly defined against one another. Indeed, Nonesuch, Henry VIII's freshly commissioned palace, designed strictly à la mode, contained no massive public hall, substituting a network of "private" chambers surrounding the privy chamber of the king. The diffusion of interests from the king's chamber—even from his privy chamber—to the chambers of his courtiers in fact became a matter of administrative concern. Even when the "hall" was not kept as a communal eating establishment presided over by the monarch or one of his officers, it was a matter of grave moment that: "sundry noblemen, gentlemen and others, doe much delight and use to dyne in corners and secret places, not repairing to the king's chamber nor hall, nor to the head officers of the household when the hall is not kept."[2]

Cromwell briefly tried to prohibit provision of "livery coals" (for cooking) to private chambers, but the attempt was a failure, for the operation of the court could no longer be contained even for the purposes of daily ceremony in the communal life of the hall—the supper parties taking place after hours in private chambers were far too important. When Wyatt laments, "They flee from me that sometime did me seek, / With naked foot stalking in my chamber" (80.1–2), he is alluding to a scene of constitutional confusion.

If one turns to other works produced by Holbein at court, one can see that his career alternates in similar ways between the public and the private, or, to be more precise, between dynastic celebrations that project the public, central, constitutional locus of the state in the king's body and other forms of representation that allow the public weal to be perceived as traversed and even determined by private interests. As the most active court painter of the 1530s and early 1540s, Holbein completed several formal, public celebrations of the Henrician court. His mural anachronistically depicting the king, his long-dead parents, and Queen Jane Seymour, for instance, although destroyed by fire at Whitehall in 1698, is suggested by the fragments of a cartoon in the National Portrait Gallery and by later copies. He also executed a magnificent woodcut for the frontispiece of the Coverdale Bible in 1535 depicting Henry presenting the Scriptures in English to his grateful Christian subjects. A delicate miniature shows Henry as Solomon receiving the Queen of Sheba (a type of the church), perhaps alluding to Henry's assumption of his title as supreme head of the church.[3]

But Holbein's career at the court of Henry VIII was devoted largely to the production of individual portraits, most of which depict the men and women who lived closest to the king in the daily routine of court life. Many of these portraits survive, and many more of the preparatory drawings "from life" (valued in their own right and collected in a "great book") also survive (in large part at Windsor Castle); they constitute what has been called the "most remarkable visual record of a royal court in European art."[4] A drawing of Sir Thomas Wyatt is among those portraits. Wyatt's torso is drawn from three-quarters, but his head is turned forward (to his right) and his portrait thus appears almost full-face. His eyes, following the movement of his head and neck, lead out of the picture and away from the artist or viewer, his eyebrows tensed just slightly together. His mouth is obscured, almost completely covered by the carefully combed hairs of his moustache and beard, with just the slightest suggestion of lips showing from beneath. The physiognomy of this portrait, like those of the rest of the group, thus draws on complex codes of social expression.

Indeed, these individual portraits make sense only when they are read as a group. Wyatt's family and close friends are also found among this intimate collection. Sir Henry Wyatt appears in a painted Holbein portrait now in the Louvre; he wears a close cap and a furred gown; his large right hand is fingering a crucifix clearly marked with the "INRI"; his left hand fingers a folded sheet of paper. Wyatt's patron Thomas Cromwell appears in a painting (a very good copy of a lost original) now in the Frick Gallery in New York, hanging just across the wall from Thomas More. Sir John Russell, whom Wyatt accompanied to Italy, appears in a drawing, as do John Poyntz (to whom Wyatt addressed two verse epistles) and Wyatt's brother-in-law Lord Cobham; Wyatt's sister and his wife are likely sitters for other portraits less surely identified.[5] And a woodcut after the Holbein drawing of Wyatt, surrounded by the large woodcut initials "T.V.," appears at the beginning of Leland's memorial volume, *Naeniae in mortem Thomae Viati*, along with a poem playing with stock themes about art and nature: "Holbenus nitida pingendi maximus arte / Effigiem expressit graphice; sed nullus Apelles / Exprimet ingenium felix animumque Viati" [Holbein, the man most skilled in the delicate art of painting, has portrayed the likeness of Wyatt in a skillful portrait. But no Apelles is fortunate enough to portray the wit and spirit of Wyatt]. Leland's elegiac evocation of lost personal uniqueness is a predictable elegiac device, of course. But it also suggests the impersonating conventions of Tudor portraiture.

The portrait, and especially the rarefied portrait miniature, a form that grew out of the work of illuminators at the royal library, emerged in the Henrician court exclusively as a product of royal patronage. Portraits are thus a typical locus for the operative confusion of personal and political power that made the Tudor court appear to swing between self-indulgent fancy and brutal efficiency, at times the easy vehicle of a warm or vicious personality, at times a political system that categorically privileged the arbitrary violence of rank. There is no question, however, that state power produced this series of portraits: there is no other reason for this particular group of people to have been drawn or painted. Holbein was Henry's artist (although he was Thomas Cromwell's first and it was Queen Anne who pushed his appointment). It was Henry's gentlemen and ladies that he painted. But they were painted as men and women. As Roy Strong has written: "There is a preoccupation with mass and form bound within rigid defining lines and an analytic rendering of both features and dress which stems from someone familiar with the ideals of renaissance scientific observation. These grave and often beguiling images have authority and dignity. Holbein's compositions render the minute surface that they cover monumental."[6] In some of the full-scale finished painted portraits, of course, there are official iconological status markers—Thomas More's chain of "ss" (a marker of Tudor royal servants) or Norfolk's ermine and staves of office.

And what makes the question of "character" interesting in these portraits is unquestionably their elite position: this is very much an art form of the royal coterie—representation that allows the importance of the sitters to be recognized. But the sitters *can* be recognized. The eyes in Holbein's portraits, and in many of them the hands—clasped, grasping a collar, playing lightly over a book or clutching it, debating, like Henry Wyatt, between the crucifix and the memorandum—provide a technical vocabulary for the representation of social codes as personal traits. The formal qualities of these paintings, then, are precisely those that enabled individual sitters to be read as "characters." No wonder it was an obsession of later owners of these portraits to name the sitters, often incorrectly, just as readers of early Tudor poetic miscellanies gave names to the authors of the poems they read.

One of the most important aspects of Wyatt's poems is the modulation of a complex rhetoric that has in common with the Tudor portrait the function of inscribing the range of social operation as "personal." I do not mean that this rhetoric was "private" in the sense that it sprang from romantic isolation or that it expressed and "belonged" to an inner self that could be sustained apart from its courtly operation. And I certainly do not mean that a consciousness called "Wyatt" fully knew what his words were saying.[7] But like the private rooms of the court, Wyatt's poems provide a space—an array of rhetorical positions—for understanding the complex social operations as if they were matters of private volition or experience or inclination, inscribing social practices upon the human subject as "character."

Thus, like the Holbein miniatures, Wyatt's shorter poems, his sonnets, epigrams, and lyrics, are also in a paradoxical sense "monumental," in that they inscribe the vast complexity, richness, and indeed confusion of the discourses circulating at court and around the court as if mediated and motivated by individual understanding and feeling: they have the same sense of challenging understatement or of rhetorical overload. The slenderness of Wyatt's poems—the sense they project of a presence greater than the brief duration of the poem itself—is indeed what one might call a technique of impersonating synecdoche or deferral. Simple exchanges between people—especially between men and women—are made to stand in for events far more complex. Voices are projected by Wyatt's rhetoric—the voices of hurt and puzzled male erotic pride, of the aggressive wit, of the eager, anxious, disappointed royal servant, of the fitful nascent evangelical conscience, of the disappointed stoic moralist. But the "presence" that these voices seems momentarily to guarantee is diffracted by their rhetoricity.

Wyatt's poetic practice, then, is a kind of rhetorical signature, a discursive formation that promises "proof" of a subject, that stands for the subject it creates, a rhetoric that makes anonymous and arbitrary conventions project and guarantee the sense of subject who is also their author. Wyatt's rhetoric, no less than his neoclassicizing monogram "T.V." of the Egerton manuscript, then, signs the subject; it promises a guarantee of the subject that it also creates as it sends out discursive signifiers of positions to be occupied. It thus "proves" not the presence of a self or of a personality but the operation of discourses that name and produce men and women. The "author" appears to "sign" his work, to guarantee its authenticity even as his field of subjectivity is inscribed—"signed", one might say, in his rhetoric.

Readers of manuscript codices in the fifteenth century often added lyrics as "autographs" that demonstrated they had read the volume or that signalled their presence to other readers. Anne Boleyn, for example, left her signature and verses in the book of hours that passed between her and Henry VIII.[8] Similarly, as the collected works of "authors" like Chaucer and Lydgate became a cultural interest in the fifteenth century, lyrics attributed to them— Chaucer's curse upon his scribe, for example—were often interspersed among their collected works to suggest a "biography" of the author.[9] In Wyatt's poems, the terms that sign the identity of the author also expose the cultural signing of the subject in rhetoric. According to the *OED*, the word *signature* itself (from the Latin "thing to be signed") emerges in its present sense of the legal inscription of identity only in the course of the sixteenth century, and it comes from the practice of submitting documents "to be signed" with the sign manual of the king—a reminder, perhaps, not just that the subject emerges here only in courtly privilege but that the authenticity of Wyatt's rhetoric is not guaranteed by the presence of the author but displaced onto the social processes that authenticate his sign, among them the emergence of human letters as a cultural field in the elite culture of early Tudor England.

Signing the Subject

Let us begin with a counterexample. Of Wyatt's surviving poems, only one seems to bear any relation to a large ceremonial public occasion: the unfinished "When Dido feasted first" or "Iopas's Song," a didactic poem about the revolution of the spheres. Though entered with painstaking revisions in Wyatt's own hand at the end of the Egerton manuscript, it is entirely differ-

ent from the rest of Wyatt's work. Both the subject matter and the setting of
the poem—it is supposed to have been sung by Iopas, Dido's bard, to welcome Aeneas—suggest its occasional origin, perhaps to celebrate the comple-
tion of the great clock at St. James Palace in a ceremony welcoming Anne of
Cleves.[10] The poem is unquestionably in Wyatt's hand, but it lacks the signature that marks so many other works attributed to Wyatt historically. For
the author it produces is not one whose authority depends upon personal
discernment, upon what Wyatt's contemporaries called his "wit." Nor does it
depend upon moral uprightness (Surrey's "an eye whose judgment none af-
fect could blind"). It depends, rather, upon reference to academic doctrine.
Its authority is didactic or perhaps even esoteric, and Wyatt does not do well
with the extensive exposition of doctrine. Even in translating some of the
longer and more philosophically discursive canzone of Petrarch, with whose
shorter lyrics Wyatt has a close sympathy, Wyatt's efforts are flattened by the
doctrinal posture. "Mine own dear enemy," for example, may refer to a personal repugnance for the adulterous woman, and "In Spain," or "So feeble is
the thread," clearly evokes Wyatt's personal longing for Elizabeth Darrell
during his extended stay abroad. But the poems have no personal authority;
Wyatt cannot sustain the philosophical dilation of his source.

I do not deny, however, that Wyatt's poems are engaged with the public
life of the court. Indeed, some of Thomas Wyatt's most difficult and moving
poems address the frequently staged scenes of the Tudor court—the hunt in
"Whoso list to hunt," for example, or the courtly entertainment in "Blame
not my lute," or the New Year's gift in "To seek each where." But even
Wyatt's work in forms that are generically "public," such as his elegy for
Thomas Cromwell ("The pillar perished is"), rescript the public trials and triumphs of the court through the rhetorical locus of personal experience.

The elegy for Cromwell provides an excellent point of departure, for it
can be situated not only in relation to the Petrarchan poem that serves as its
model, but to the documents surviving from the historical moment that it
transcribes. Cromwell was executed in 1541 following the collapse of his
dynastic strategies and courtly friendships in the wake of Henry VIII's repugnance for Anne of Cleves—a failed dynastic marriage that itself illustrates a peculiar slippage between the politics of the early modern state and
the "subject" that it interpellates ideologically, for the king too was a "subject," a "man" like his fellow courtiers, and he found the bride that he had
been betrothed to as the body of state physically repellent. Wyatt's own career, of course, was placed in peril by Cromwell's poor choice of Henry's
marriage partner, for Cromwell had been his patron and indeed more than
once his savior since the early 1530s. Wyatt thus turns to a sonnet Petrarch

had written lamenting the deaths of both Laura and of his patron Cardinal
Giovanni di Colonna, whose name, meaning "column," provides the conceit
for the first lines. Wyatt drops the mention of Laura, but he retains the broken column (an emblem of disappointed hope) even without the punning
topical allusion:

> The pillar perished is whereto I leant,
> The strongest stay of mine unquiet mind;
> The like of it no man again can find—
> From east to west still seeking though he went—
> To mine unhap, for hap away hath rent
> Of all my joy the very bark and rind,
> And I, alas, by chance am thus assigned
> Dearly to mourn till death do it relent.
>   (29.1–8)

Taking these lines about the fortunes of the bereft speaker as its cue, Wyatt's
poem then literally writes in its author, pen in hand:

> But since that thus it is by destiny,
> What can I more but have a woeful heart,
> My pen in plaint, my voice in woeful cry,
> My mind in woe, my body full of smart,
> And I myself myself always to hate
> Till dreadful death do cease my doleful state?
>   (29.9–14)

What makes this imitation remarkable is that the drama of the author's suffering and the anticipation of his death pathetically displaces the death of
Cromwell. Petrarch's sonnet commends the lost patron and lover, dwelling
upon the preciousness and fragility of the objects men treasure:

> Tolto m'hai, Morte, il mio doppio tesauro
> che me fea viver lieto e gire altero;
> e ristorar no'l può terra né impero
> né gemma oriental, né forza d'auro.
>
> Ma se consentimento è destino,
> che poso io più se no aver l'alma trista,
> umida gli occhi sempre, e'l viso chino?

O nostra vita ch'è sì bella in vista,
com' perde agelmente in un matino
quel che'n molti anni a gran pena s'acquista.

You have taken from me, O Death, my double treasure that made me live glad and
walk proudly; neither land nor empire can restore it, nor orient gem, nor the power of
gold.

But since it is the intent of destiny, what can I do except have my soul sad, my eyes always wet, and my face bent down?

Oh our life that is so beautiful to see, how easily it closes in one morning what has
been acquired with great difficulty over many years.[11]

Wyatt expands upon the pathos of loss as experienced by the author—and it
is a loss that occasions self-loathing. I say "author" here because, rhetorically,
the speaker of this poem speaks as its author, pen in hand: this is a poem that
foregrounds writing down feelings in conventions that we call "literary." Indeed, the scene of writing displaces the scene of execution and the irreversible
political process that led to it onto the emotive grammar of mourning.

To the reader today, perhaps, this suicidal grief seems excessive. But it is a
common gesture in the cultural productions of the early Tudor court, an idiom made "genuine" by the context of noble Roman moralism and the aristocratic male narcissism that appropriated its gestures. Surrey lamented the
death of his childhood companion Henry Fitzroy, earl of Richmond (Henry
VIII's illegitimate son, married to Surrey's sister and hence a further dynastic
tie to the royal family), in "When Windesor walles" (Jones, no. 11) with similar histrionics. Surrey's atavistic poem places the speaker upon the walls of
Windsor Castle where he and Richmond had lived when Surrey had enjoyed
the pride and power of being his preceptor, now finding himself alone lamenting the death of this boy who as his friend was also the pledge of the
Howard dynasty. The loss of this beloved threatens the security of Surrey's
sense of identity: "And I half bent to throw me down withal." So too Wyatt
felt as something "personal" or even "essential" the loss of Cromwell and all
the complex social and political accidents that are bound up in it both as
cause of his fall and the loss issuing from it. Petrarch had conflated the loss of
Colonna and of his beloved Laura. And in the language of service, Cromwell
too was a beloved friend, "of all my joy the very bark and rind," words taken
seamlessly from the romantic context of Chaucer's *Troilus*.[12] Within the
emotional circuits of this love the death of a patron means the mournful suffering of a client. Wyatt's feelings of responsibility, the guilt and grief of sur-

vival after love is severed in death—they were all part of the script. And so too, I suspect, were his poems. After all, Cromwell had extended his love to men humanistically inclined because their way of rewriting experience was so often convenient: the pursuit of friendship is a central humanist trope.

Cromwell's feelings in the last moments of his life, described in a contemporary Spanish account, are similarly loaded onto his "great love": "Among the gentlemen around the scaffold Cromwell caught sight of Master Wyatt, and he called to him and said, 'Gentle Wyatt, God be with you, and I pray you to pray God for me': There had always been great love between him and this Master Wyatt. And Wyatt could not answer him for his tears came too fast."[13] According to a contemporary account in English (a commonplace book kept by Richard Cox, bishop of Ely) that corroborates this sometimes fanciful Spanish chronicle, Cromwell's last words upon the scaffold were addressed to Wyatt: "& he turned him abowt & sayed Farewell Wyat. / & gentell Wiat praye for me."[14] As Cromwell stages his last scene, he reaches out to his friend in a gesture that stands for their shared histories. It includes the memory, of course, of Wyatt being saved during the bloody days of Queen Anne's fall. It assumes the complex ties of service and patronage. It looks forward to the avalanche of disenfranchisement that would follow his death. In the single word "gentle" it adumbrates (and perhaps ironizes) the whole shared set of courtly values. And Cromwell's bidding for Wyatt's prayers transfers the discourse to an eschatological frame of reference that stops just short of claiming self-justification in the eyes of God. The farewell and the bidding of prayers operate as a synecdoche, then, for what could not be said. Like Thomas More's famous jest to the lieutenant of the Tower escorting him up the steps to the scaffold—"I pray you, master lieutenant, see me safe up, and for my coming down let me shift for myself"—Cromwell's last words draw their pathos and their complex and devastating irony out of personal address. No wonder Wyatt cried. Cromwell had given him the cue. In another age men like Nathan Hale might be supposed to die invoking moral principle alone, but for Cromwell, Wyatt, More, as later for Sir Philip Sidney ("thy necessity is greater than mine") and for the histories that record their last scenes, what makes the theological and moral abstractions operative is not an Enlightenment faith in an orderly providence but their engagement in a scene written by Fortune and perceived as taking place in a conversation of friends.

Wyatt touches upon the staging of such a final scene himself in an extraordinary poem in the Devonshire manuscript, "Who list his wealth and ease retain," written after the bloody days that had brought the execution of Anne's alleged lovers, arrested along with Wyatt, on Tower hill, and the beheading of the queen herself at the Tower, where Wyatt, inside his cell, awaited news of his own fate:

> Who list his wealth and ease retain,
> Himself let him unknown contain.
> Press not to fast in at that gate
> Where the return stands by disdain,
> For sure, *circa Regna tonat.*
>
> The high mountains are blasted oft
> When the low valley is mild and soft.
> Fortune with Health stands at debate.
> The fall is grievous from aloft.
> And sure, *circa Regna tonat.*
>
> These bloody days have broken my heart.
> My lust, my youth did them depart,
> And blind desire of estate.
> Who hastes to climb seeks to revert.
> Of truth, *circa Regna tonat.*
>
> The bell tower showed me such sight
> That in my head sticks day and night.
> There did I learn out of a grate,
> For all favour, glory, or might,
> That yet *circa Regna tonat.*
>
> By proof, I say, there did I learn:
> Wit helpeth not defence too yerne,
> Of innocency to pleade or prate.
> Bear low, therfore, give God the stern,
> For sure, *circa Regna tonat.*
>
> (123.1–25)

The poem finds its stoic philosophical argument stanza by stanza, slowly and sparingly recalling a painful memory in the barest and most brutal terms. It is the same story, of course, that Bonner had thought Wyatt's obsession—"was not that a prety sending of me ambassadour first to put me into the Tower."[15] It is situated with a stark realism ("out of a grate") at its origin in the repugnant imprisonment in the Tower, and the bloody sight that the speaker has seen is useful now as a moral "proof" that he has learned, presented as a lesson to one "who would his wealth and ease retain." The power that the speaker has experienced is absolute; there is no room for pleading innocent; one must simply stay away from the center of power or else submit to its arbitrary judgments. This is a common moral lesson of stoic virtue, but what sets it in motion in this poem is the sense evoked of a personal origin as the deliberative rhetoric of the speaker produces, stanza by stanza, a repugnant memory as "proof."

The speaker of the poem protects himself from the memory by withdrawal, but his freedom is precarious; his vision is filtered through a grate. Indeed, the poem is headed in the Blage manuscript by a title that elaborately figures the name of the author into a brief allegory:

> *V. Innocentia*
> *Veritas Viat Fides*
> *Circumdederunt me inimici mei*
>
> *Innocence*
> *Truth Wyatt Faith*
> *My enemies have surrounded me*[16]

Wyatt's name (Viat) appears "surrounded" not only by the virtues of innocence, truth, and faith, but also by his "enemies," an allusion to Psalm 17. And it is by "naming" himself, by situating this stoic lesson of withdrawal in a biographical memory, a scene attached to his person, that Wyatt has achieved the impersonating rhetorical power of his poem. And it is also through this personal exposure that he has put at risk some of his own themes. For his moral center, his inner self, is, in the graphic image of the title, a name encircled by words. And just as the graphics are dangerous (just who does surround Wyatt, his enemies, his virtues, or both? or are the virtues that would keep him in such a situation in a sense his enemies?), so too is its relation to the text from Seneca that provides the first two stanzas and the refrain: *circa regna tonat*. The phrase comes from the chorus of the *Phaedra* (1123–1140) that follows the long recital by a messenger of the tragic death of Hippolytus:

> Iuppiter alto vicina petit;
> non capit umquam magnos motus
> humilis tecti plebeia domus.
> circa regna tonat.

Jupiter is attacking places from on high. The modest dwelling and the humble roof are never touched by great tumults. He thunders around thrones. (my translation)

Who thunders around the throne in Wyatt's poem? Is he the same as the God to whom one is urged to "give the stern"? If so, there is an easy reading: God is just. Or is the subject of *circa regna tonat* an arbitrary tyrant? And just how close to the story of this tragic ancient household would one wish this very literary poem to go—Theseus who murdered his first wife Antiope and married Phaedra?

Currency, Authority, and Authorities

The poetry of Wyatt and the other courtly makers has sometimes been related to the orality and performative aspects of English court culture. In a memorable phrase C. S. Lewis once associated Wyatt's lyrics with "a little music after supper."[17] Wyatt's lyrics did become part of the Tudor oral entertainment—they continued to be set to music throughout the century, although not necessarily by gentlemen like Wyatt of the inner circle. Julia Boffey has demonstrated that the two large songbooks surviving from the court of Henry VIII contain some courtly lyrics, but that they "were probably designed more for the use of the singing-men of the Chapel Royal—clerks— than for that of illustrious courtiers, or of the king himself."[18] As John Stevens has suggested, there is no compelling evidence that Wyatt wrote with music in mind or intended his poems to be performed. Wyatt's poetry is not strictly oral, but in Stevens's words "idealized talk."[19] Indeed, one of the qualities that makes Wyatt an inaugural poet is the insistent "written-ness" of his work, its rhetorical engagement with its own textual scene of invention. We do not know whether Wyatt's poems were sung or recited in courtly settings. We do know, however, that Wyatt's work circulated in poetic manuscripts; that it was copied by many hands; that the poems in the Egerton, Arundel, Devonshire, and Blage manuscripts were read as texts and through texts. At one point, for example, one of the hands of the Devonshire manuscript has copied out verses from Thynne's 1532 printed edition of Chaucer. In another manuscript, a scribe has copied out the Italian source of an epigram. Underneath the Egerton text of "Madame withouten many words" is entered (late in the sixteenth century) a poem headed "Answer" and beginning "Of few words sir you seem to be," a poem in the person of a woman and perhaps written by a woman along with a series of entries in the same hand.[20]

In the Cromwell elegy as in his Horatian verse epistle "Mine own John Poyntz," Wyatt imagines himself "at his book" and "amongst my muses where I read and rhyme," (49. 81, 101) the self-conscious pose of a public man withdrawing to letters in a moment of adversity.[21] And while Wyatt's poetry is rarely bookish, it is consistently engaged—consciously and unconsciously—

with the ways in which texts intersect, overlap, and contradict. H. A. Mason has long been making the argument that Wyatt's best work represented the humanist project of translation. And Wyatt's most influential recent readers, Thomas Greene and Stephen Greenblatt, emphasize in different ways the complex semiotic relations that give Wyatt's poetry its cultural resonance. Greenblatt is interested in how the language of Wyatt's poetry "implicates" and "suspends" the terms through which the culture of the court is written, in how Wyatt's poetry finds its "roots not in the quirks of a complex personality. . . but in the conflicting cultural codes that fashion identity in the Tudor court lyric." And Greene's study of Wyatt in the rich cultural context of renaissance imitation explores Wyatt's active heuristic engagement with the alterity of his classical and Petrarchan subtexts, tellingly illustrated by Greene in his dense reading of the dialectical nuances of translation in "Stand whoso list," Wyatt's imitation of a passage from Seneca's *Thyestes*.[22] Greene places more emphasis than Greenblatt on Wyatt's artistic control in mediating his sources; Greenblatt stresses the "internal distance" or "gap between discourse and intention"[23] that allows the containing ideology to be seen from the inside. Like Greenblatt, I should like to stress the larger cultural implication of Wyatt's production; and following Greene and Mason, I should also like to emphasize how much the cultural production of Wyatt's subjectivity is bound up by its very "written-ness," its literariness, in problems of literary economy, of cultural currency and authority.

In figuring the death of an "author," both Leland and Surrey had placed a premium upon form and style as they celebrated the inauguration of an English literary history. In Surrey's words, Wyatt possessed "a hand that taught what might be sayd in ryme," and Leland claimed that he had "taught the nobility how to sing in different forms." To them, as to the Elizabethans, Wyatt and Surrey were, in the words of Puttenham's *Arte of English Poesie*, the first of "a new company of courtly makers" that "sprong up" at the end of the reign of Henry VIII and "greatly pollished our rude and homely maner of vulgar Poesie," having travelled into Italy and returned with the "sweete and stately measures and stile of the Italian poesie."[24] Puttenham's words are echoed by many others, and they are compelling, for Puttenham is not only speaking about mere poetic decor, but also about the complex social function that is bound up in the emergence of secular, vernacular letters as a cultural category. The emphasis on form and style that marks the inauguration of modern letters in England as elsewhere in northern Europe is, I believe, the theoretical signal of the impersonating rhetoric that I have been alluding to. For it was in part through his relation to "authors," the literary authorities that were being given cultural currency through their fashionable circulation in court culture, that Thomas Wyatt, like his French contemporary Clémont Marot, for example, negotiated his own position as an author, above all in relation to Petrarch, whose sonnets he was the first to translate into English, and whose collective and shifting influence on generations of Petrarchism provides a medium for the assimilation of vernacular tradition and classical letters in the emerging nations of Europe as a new elite subjectivity emerged, scripted in part through these changing conventions.

I place Petrarch in the foreground here, perhaps ahistorically, only because in the backward glance of narrative historiography his example seems to have been the medium or cultural vehicle through which so many discourses were enabled to pass. I shall look again at Wyatt and the Petrarchan cognitive complex in chapter 4. But I do not mean to slight other authorities. For Wyatt wrote himself and was written in relation to many different discourses. Not all of them were strictly "literary" as we use that term, for sixteenth-century letters extended across fields we today would call philosophy, history, political theory, sociology, psychology, and linguistics. Wyatt was, for example, like most gentlemen of his generation, influenced (whether he read them or not) by the constitutional thinking of Fortescue and other theorists of commonwealth and common law in fifteenth-century England who theorized the state and the legal subject in relation to one another. Looking in particular at the *bonae litterae* of Wyatt's particular scene of reading and writing, I believe that he negotiated his rhetorical practices in relation to Serafino d'Aquila, for example, a favorite of the continental court; to Luigi Alamanni, a Florentine exile at the court of Francis I; to Chaucer, whose works were being reproduced for courtly consumption (the 1532 edition of Chaucer's works was edited by Richard Thynne, clerk of the king's kitchen); to the humanist rhetoric, both theoretical and applied, Latin and vernacular, that was spilling from the printing presses of early modern Europe and invading the reading and writing consciousness of the elite; to the Roman moralists, to Horace, and to Ovid, to the many classical authorities that were being invested with new meaning as court culture selectively appropriated the "human letters" of the new learning to shape the secular authority of a vernacular national literature; to the stern magisterial voices of Luther and the other reformers, telling the literate subjects of early modern Europe what they already knew, that their faith—another (theological) word for subjectivity—was written in words that they spoke and read.

One of the Continental forms that Wyatt inaugurated was the *strambotto*, an epigrammatic stanza made popular by Serafino d'Aquila in Italy and sweeping the court of Francis I.[25] Looking at Wyatt's adventures with this form provides an appropriate place to examine the cultural entitlement that formal invention could enable. The eight lines of the strambotto (generally rhymed *a b a b a b c c*) and, in particular, its tendency to break syntactically into distiches made it an excellent medium for rapid rhetorical progression and closure. This short, versatile form thus provided a vehicle not only for the conceits of fifteenth-century Petrarchism, but for the range of occasional and epideictic performance licensed in the neoclassical epigram: poems of compliment and complaint, poems of greeting and farewell, gifts, curses, and thank-you's—social uses exemplified in abundance in the Latin epigrams of Thomas More, of Wyatt's friend John Leland, or of Nicolas de Bourbon, the distinguished French protestant scholar and poet who spent several years at the English court in the 1530s. The epigram could move back and forth between acute topical reference and grand literary allusion, between close classical imitation and the appropriation of homely proverbs—an appropriate working space for the cultural rivalry of the new learning or of vernacular letters and their classical cultural model. It was thus a form excellently suited for performative wit, a species of literary competition that clearly adumbrates the rhetorical display and competition of courtly politics. In the overstocked treasury of epigrammatic literature, the courtier could find suitable words for any occasion, a ready-made voice into which he could insert himself; a forceful opinion he could borrow; a sense of humor he could count on to draw polite laughter. An epigrammatic form like the strambotto was thus enfranchised as a perfect vehicle for the representation of social exchange. It was cultural currency indeed, and it moved fast.

Even at its most static and superficial the strambotto could speak the language of self-promotion. It was a form of assertive wit, very much like the *facetia*, or merry tale—another genre at which Wyatt excelled, writing to Henry VIII, for example, that the diplomatic subtleties swirling around negotiations with Francis I reminded him of the "tale of the Welshe man, when he was in danger on the see, that vowd a taper as bigg as the mast, and when he came on land payd a litill candell to our Lady with that he offrd her to hang hym [if] euer she toke hym on the see againe."[26] A witty tale like this deflects from social tension to assert the personal power of the speaker as an intermediary; it provides a graceful discursive opportunity to forget. It may point an intellectual irony, but it provides a social cover; it can mask failure or confusion with the shared joy of rhetorical empowerment.

This kind of rhetorical mastery is not always vigorous and earthy in Wyatt's work. It appears, for example, in the delicate social nuances of a poem little discussed (perhaps because it is so atypical of the "manly" Wyatt we are accustomed to producing) about a stolen glove and a lost heart:

What needeth these threnning words and wasted wind?
All this cannot make me restore my prey.
To rob your good, iwis, is not my mind,
Nor causeless your fair hand did I display.
Let Love be judge or else whom next we meet
That may both hear what you and I can say:
"She took from me a heart and I a glove from her.
Let us see now if th'one be worth th'other."

(40)

Surrey could well have written a poem like this. Its thematic play of loss and seizure has little thematic import beyond the enactment of an elegant social stance that makes a game out of the turning of the tables in the give and take of erotic play. The casualness and confidence of the appeal not just to Cupid but to "whom next we meet," the pride of uncovering or "displaying" the lady's "fair hand," the male insolence of the closing couplet, which asks for "more" from the lady to recompense the loss of his heart—these are the markers of erotic elegy and a sophisticated and irreverent neoclassical style.

But the rhetorical mastery of the neoclassical mode made available to Wyatt in the strambotto is played out in a widely differentiated register of stylistic modalities. "A face that should content me wondrous well" is a tender poem of compliment, perhaps addressed to Elizabeth Darrell, expressing a hopeful proposal of marriage, with only the edge of irony or doubt slipping into the conditionals of its last lines: "With wit, and these, might chance I might be tied / And knit again the knot that should not slide" (67. 9–10). "Right true it is," on the other hand, is a bitter diatribe against political backstabbing. And then too there is the grim irony of Wyatt's poem about a suicidal mix-up, a stock matter for the turning of epigrammatic wit:

For shamefast harm of great and hateful need,
In deep desire as did a wretch go
With ready cord out of his life to speed,
His stumbling foot did find an hoard, lo,
Of gold, I say, where he prepared this deed,
And in exchange he left the cord tho.
He that had hid the gold and found it not,
Of that he found he shaped his neck a knot.

(51)

Confident poems of mastery such as this one can expose the anxieties that they would mask. This is a fatal irony that allows laughter at the expense of defeated expectations and sudden turns in fortune, a polite courtly form of gallows humor that deflects the dangers of the "slipper top of world's estate" (49.1).

These can be smooth poems, to be sure. But the rhetorical motivation of these poems is impure. Indeed, the interest in the macabre that motivates some epigrams masks unspeakable repression and fear. I am thinking, for example, of the pathetic infanticide who is portrayed in a poem that appears in Egerton MS. 2711 in Wyatt's hand, an apparent translation from an Italian strambotto based on Josephus.[27] A Jewish mother is supposed to have killed and eaten her newborn son during a famine when Jerusalem was under seige:

> In doubtful breast whilst motherly pity
> With furious famine standeth at debate,
> Saith th'Hebrew mother, "O child unhappy,
> Return thy blood where thou hadst milk of late.
> Yield me those limbs that I made unto thee
> And enter there where thou were generate.
> For of one body against all nature
> To another must I make sepulture."
>
> (45)

As Muir and Thomson note,[28] Wyatt "throws the emphasis on to the mother's doubt, and, instead of describing her as utterly pitiless . . . creates a conflict between her pity and her hunger." It is possible, of course, to mitigate the poem by thematizing its image as morally instructive, as a paradox of life and death or an example of "pity" or of the "inhumanity" of war or the insolence of natural disaster. But the obscene interest of the poem rests in the scene of violation, in the equation of female sexuality with death, above all in the defensive inscription of the maternal cannibalism as incestuous: "Return thy blood . . . Yield me those limbs . . . And enter there where thou wert generate." Just what does rhetoric like this have mastery over?

Similarly, the lascivious wit of Wyatt's erotic strambotti can often exceed the terms of the rhetorical power that they assert, as it does for example in "She sat and sewed," or in the riddle Wyatt poses that depends upon sexual "knowledge":

> A lady gave me a gift she had not
> And I received her gift which I took not.
> She gave it willingly, yet she would not;
> And I received it, albeit I could not.
> If she gave it me, I force not.

> If she take again, she cares not.
> Construe what is this and tell not,
> For I am fast sworn I may not.
>
> (63)

The riddle contains its own answer, the word "not" or "naught" that ends each line, referring obliquely to the illicit "naughty" zone of female sexuality, the "O" or "naught" of the vagina. The speaker thus answers the riddle he poses, tells the secret he has sworn to keep, and continues to pun upon the "double standard" of sexuality that the assertive wit of the poem depends upon, playing the inscription of the woman's body as both a "nothing," an empty vessel, a trifle that can be had at will, against its inscription as a virginity, an untouchable zone, that the male speaker can "not" or should "not" possess, a precious flower that must not be plucked. Wyatt's style has often been called "manly," and sometimes equated with Donne; this poem surely has something in common with the voyeuristic Donne of the elegies, as it does with the erotic wit of Martial or Ovid. But it is a manliness that is often overeager, and perhaps overcompensating, transferring the "naught" of its own inadequacy ("And I received it, albeit I could not") onto the "naught" of the woman. Like one of Wyatt's other well-known riddles, which asks "What word is that which changeth not / Though it be turned and made in twain?" and responds, "It is mine answer [that is, Anna, sir], God it wot, / And eke the causer of my pain" (54.1–4) this poem "masters" the fiction of the refusing woman only by distorting her (or her body) in wit.

I am tempted to continue to explore Wyatt's lascivious wit, discussing, for example, "The furious gun," the poem in which Wyatt compares the implosion of his broken heart to the firing of a cannon, but another interest of Wyatt's epigrammatic poems comes from the way Wyatt "exposes" himself—partially and teasingly—as the biographical conventions of voyage poems, poems based on historical exampla, and poems of stoic withdrawal from adversity provoke unforeseen moments of discursive disjunction. Even poems that seem most true "to life" such as the moving complaints written from political disgrace are after all examples of literary occasions. The practice of withdrawing to the muses in personal adversity is automatic; again and again in his career, Wyatt will turn from political defeat to poetic composition—and find a model waiting for him. This strambotto, perhaps written in 1541, for example, is translated almost line for line out of Serafino:

> He is not dead that sometime hath a fall.
> The sun returneth that was under the cloud.
> And when Fortune hath spit out all her gall
> I trust good luck to me shall be allowed.
> For I have seen a ship in haven fall
> After the storm hath broke both mast and shroud.
> And eke the willow that stoopeth with the wind
> Doth rise again and greater wood doth bind.
>
>   (42)

The translation is faultless. Line for line, Wyatt has found the idiom to translate the unyielding voice of his source. He can impersonate the composure, patience, and unbending will that the genre calls for with grace and vigor. Line by line this poem swells syntactically, moving from the one-line sentences of determination in the opening lines to grow into a more complex syntax of resistance as the speaker figures his resilience and faith in the second half of the poem.

But the poems do not always work out so neatly. From Spain Wyatt wrote an enigmatic epigram about the conflict between "intimate" feelings and his "official service": a conflict between "public" and "private" that is played out in his "person." The poem begins with an allusion that Petrarch had used to begin *Rime* 103, alluding to Hannibal's well-known failure to take advantage of his victory over the Romans at Cannae during the Second Punic war: "Vinse Anibàl, et non seppe usar poi/ben la vittoriosa sua ventura" [Hannibal was victorious, but he did not know later how to make good use of his victorious fortune]. Whether Wyatt was working directly from Petrarch or from a later imitation, he uses the example of Hannibal to suggest his own frustration as an ambassador. The poem is addressed from Monzòn in Spain, where Wyatt had been caught in 1537, pursuing the hopeless task of preventing Charles V and Francis I from agreeing to a truce with Milan that would put England at risk (by freeing France to turn against England). As he wrote to Cromwell, desperately begging to be recalled: "I ame at the wall."[28] But it also alludes to Wyatt's own personal "conquest" of Elizabeth Darrell and his longing to return to her in England:

> Of Carthage he, that worthy warrior,
> Could overcome but could not use his chance.
> And I likewise, of all my long endeavour,
> The sharp conquest though fortune did advance,
> Could not it use. The hold is given over
> I unpossessed. So hangeth in balance

> Of war my peace, reward of all my pain.
> At Monzòn thus I restless rest in Spain.
>
> (46)

The overlapping terms here thus confuse the interests of the state (conquest in war, diplomatic advantage, peace treaty) with those of the individual subject who is supposed to embody it (conquest in love, success in diplomatic career, peace of mind). And what is potentially most unnerving here is thus the unsettling of the very person that the rhetoric projects: a person traversed and tormented by the many circuits of agency he operates in. This is the contradiction that Surrey picks up on when he ironically echoes Wyatt's phrase "thus I restless rest in Spain" in his epitaph: "Wyatt resteth here that quick could never rest."

The great promise of this poem is that its contradictory unsettledness—the distance between its confident voice and its riddling contradictions—seems to deploy a logic of concealment, a promise of a subjectivity that guarantees this utterance, that secures its incompleteness, that answers its enigma. It is for this paradoxical play on emptiness and fullness that I also like to read "Tagus, farewell," a poem that I continue to admire after countless readings because I cannot fully understand it. It appears in Wyatt's hand in Egerton MS. 2711, with the same title as the long canzone, "So feeble is the thread." The speaker of both poems longs to return to his beloved. In the canzone, the speaker observes the slow progress of the sun ("westward the sun from out the east scant doth show his light") and wishes to overcome slow time and distant space: "I know not how to attain the wings that I require, / To lift my weight that it might fly to follow my desire" (76.17, 25–26). The figuration of the epigram is similar, and, it is similar also to another Petrarchan passage, which I believe was in fact its source. The speaker bids farewell to the Tagus river in Spain, and wishes for "wings . . . of mighty love" to carry him home:

> Tagus, farewell, that westward with thy streams
> Turns up the grains of gold already tried,
> With spur and sail for I go seek the Thames,
> Gainward the sun that shew'th her wealthy pride
> And, to the town which Brutus sought by dreams,
> Like bended moon doth lend her lusty side.
> My king, my country, alone for whom I live,
> Of mighty love the wings for this me give.

The poem is embroidered with neoclassical conventions and Petrarchan allusion. The figure of the golden Tagus is ubiquitous; it occurs, for example, in Chaucer's Boethius and in the chorus from Seneca's *Thyestes* from which Wyatt translated "Stand whoso list." The story of Brutus's founding of Troynovant at London is from Geoffrey of Monmouth, whose Trojan legend had new currency under the Tudor ambitions of empire. The poem is in genre a protempticon, a poem written on the eve of a departure; it is also a "river" poem, a common epigrammatic type that is worked into Petrarchan literature, a subtle figuration of place in a continuing Petrarchan allegory of landscape. And behind the poem lies an exquisite and evasive sonnet of Petrarch's, in which the speaker, travelling in body at least down the Po, addresses the river god, proclaiming that his spirit is beating his wings and flying against the stream toward the "golden leaves" ("l'aurea fronde") that signify his beloved Laura:

> Re degli altri, superbo altro fiume
> ch'ncontri'l sol quando e' ne mena 'l giorno
> e'n ponente abandoni unpiú bel lume:
>
> tu te ne vai col mio mortal sul corno;
> l'altro, ocverto d'amorose piume,
> torna volando al suo dolce soggiorno.

King of the other rivers, proud and haughty river, you who greet the sun when he brings us the day and leave behind a more beautiful light in the west:

you carry on your horn [corno, i.e., crescent] what is mortal of me; the other part, covered with feathers of love, returns flying to his sweet dwelling.[29]

Wyatt would seem to pick up obliquely on the sexual play of Petrarch's images. For Petrarch subtly "cuckolds" the masculine strength of this river god with his "crescent" or "horned" course as the speaker's spirit, with its wings of love, flies against the stream. But Wyatt's poem is in the conditional: his wings are not yet set on the contrary course. And the allusion to Brutus too is conditional, for while Wyatt enjoys the cultural power that the Trojan origin of London carries, he also brings in the uncertainty of the exile who "sought" his new Troy "by dreams." And his river is female. Picking up the allusion to the "crescent" or "horned" moon of the Po, as he curves toward the east (that is, away from his Laura), Wyatt playfully contrasts the spent, tried gold of the Tagus, its waters already caught by the sunlight as it flows from east to west, to the strong course of the Thames, which flows east displaying her "wealthy pride," her outbound shipping, the wealth of the rich port of London, toward the fresh light of the sun, while she saves the "lusty" inside of her crescent for the city and its nights of pleasure. The sexual vigor and longing are clear. But what is fascinating is the overlay between sexual pride and the pride of an Englishman; between love for a distant beloved and love for "My king, my country, alone for whom I live." The sexuality and the love of country seem to be figures for one another. Later readers were uncomfortable with this poem. Tottel changes the final couplet: "My king, my countrey, I seke for whom I liue, / Oh mighty Ioue the windes for this me geve."[30] For that is the other vulnerable spot in the Egerton version, the blasphemous thought that one could live for king, for country, for love, but not for God.

There is a riddling quality to poems like "Tagus farewell": they promise to be confessional, but they withhold more than they tell. Wyatt enjoyed riddles like "What word is that," of course, and they are another signal of his taste for humanist games of linguistic exposure and concealment. H. A. Mason has recently demonstrated the origins of Wyatt's riddle of the cannon, "Vulcan begat me," in "Bombarda," a fable by Pandolfo Collenuccio, a humanist secretary in the service of Ercole d'Este of Ferrara.[31] And as Mason suggests, there too Wyatt plays with the suture between the personal and the public. The cannon is thus a figure for temper (or perhaps, I might add, for sexual energy, as in "The furious gun") as well as an image of public military might and destruction. It is just the suture that I should like to look at in another puzzle poem, "Accused though I be," which spells out the name of a prominent lady of court in an acrostic: it names either Anne Stanhope, the wife of Sir Michael Stanhope, a Nottinghamshire courtier and a partisan of Edward Seymour, or their daughter, also Anne Stanhope, who became Seymour's wife in the late 1530s. The bold capitals of the anagram in this poem demonstrate not the male will to possess, as does the "Anna" of the palindrome in "What word is that," but the radical instability of the terms of love and friendship. This poem names its lady in a plea that involves almost unrecoverably the overlay of personal feeling, patronage, and faction:

> Accused though I be without desert,
> None can it prove, yet ye believe it true,
> Nor never yet, since that ye had my heart,
> Entended I to be false or untrue.
> Sooner would I of death sustain the smart
> Than break one thing of that I promised you.
> Accept therefore my service in good part.

None is alive that ill tongues can eschew.
Hold them as false and let us not depart
Our friendship old in hope of any new.
Put not thy trust in such as use to feign
Except thou mind to put thy friends to pain.

The voice layers the patience of the exile and the tenderness and hurt of the spurned lover; it is impossible to tell whether the poem concerns grave legal charges brought against the speaker, the political dangers of one of Wyatt's falls from grace, or simply the slander of ill tongues about some possibly trivial matter. Is the occasion a tiff or an affair of state? Is this a case of misunderstanding among friends, or of betrayal? Is it a polite and apologetic reprimand? A desperately hurt plea? The speaker who so eloquently projects patience and understanding despite his own hurt feelings and betrayal, who seems to project a presence in his poem, withdraws into his rhetoric. The signature that this poem appears to write, the voice that it momentarily embodies, recedes into the name of another, and Anne Stanhope remains an oblique code: an acrostic that spells a name, but does not produce a person.

Chapter Three
Letters and Voices

"Mine own John Poyntz," "My mother's maids," and "A spending hand" appear close together in the Egerton manuscript; they stand out as a group in other early Tudor manuscripts and in "Tottel's Miscellany." There is no reason to suppose that they must have been composed at the same time. But they do constitute a generic group. They are all written in the fluid and versatile terza rima of the penitential psalms; they are all formally addressed to fellow courtiers as verse epistles; and they all carry the clear generic signal of the Horatian epistolary style, the independent moral voice of the gentleman in repose. As Stephen Greenblatt has commented, following generations of sympathetic readers, these verse epistles mark a "crucial moment in English letters."[1] Here Wyatt discovered and domesticated a voice that would speak the aspirations (and mask the anxieties) of the English establishment for centuries to come. Indeed, it was cultural productions like Wyatt's verse epistles and Thomas Elyot's *Book of the Governor,* works providing imaginary form for the complex personal polity of the Henrician court, that inaugurated the institution of the gentleman—the Wyatts and their neighbors in the courtly suburb of Kent are prime examples—as a fluid cultural category for the "ruling" classes of royal administration, effectively writing the name of a gentleman (authorized by the Royal College of Arms) over otherwise important and operative differences in status, patronage, wealth, occupation, family, sect, and ideology.

These poems are often called satires. Two of them have analogues in Horace's *sermones*; there are several echoes of Juvenal and Persius; and all three present satiric attacks upon the vices of the powerful. As these allusions suggest, the cultural power that poems like these obtained in Tudor England was surely collective, for even their neoclassical novelty depended in part upon well-formed habits of reading. Works like Wyatt's verse epistles enjoy the sanction of an oppositional stance that recalls not only classical satire but the social "complaint" and the Boethian contempt of the world—stances that neoclassical forms such as this join, transform, and repossess in early modern

England. There are also important relations between these poems and other epideictic forms favored by Wyatt, the epigram and the *strambotto*.

Yet their generic status as verse epistles—epistolary satires, if you will—is important not simply for its neoclassical novelty, fashion, and authority, but precisely because they are formally letters from one person to another. Much in these poems depends upon their mode of address. In them, a gentleman addresses gentlemen by means of a literary recreation that plays dangerously over the complex and contradictory discourses that one can also read in their official correspondence. As a diplomat Wyatt was, I have suggested, charged with being the surrogate of his king and with seeing through kings, with being a wit attractive to royal fancy and a compliant royal servant. In assuming the voice of the gentleman in repose or retirement, Wyatt speaks an analogous cultural contradiction, for if the power of the gentleman is indeed "personal"—his to offer or to withdraw at will—it operates only in the overlapping networks of clientage and obligation that service at the royal court sustains. His status requires engagement; it is confirmed by society, just as his privilege is confirmed by the royal College of Arms. His freedom as an individual is intricately bound up with the production of the court as the center of the early modern state. Thus, a gentleman's retirement from service, like an ambassador's witty one-upmanship with princes, is rhetorical. I do not, however, mean to suggest by calling this retirement rhetorical that it is not real, or that it does not work. I believe that the rhetoric that allows these Horatian letters to speak the voice of the English gentleman performs cultural work of analysis and defense that is critical indeed. Through works such as these the subjects of early Tudor England came to terms with the positions into which the shifting terms of their changing culture were placing them. And the "voice" that is so critical in effecting this cultural work is best understood not simply as personal but as produced socially in letters and by letters. In his verse epistles, Wyatt and his readers could find in the uncertain circuits of rhetoric a means of tentatively engaging, both consciously and unintentionally, the very terms upon which they are obliged to operate. The "voice" that "speaks" in the letters exposes the "letters" of the discourses that allow it to speak. And whether or not all three of the satires date from Wyatt's imprisonment in the Tower and his house arrest at home following the fall of Anne Boleyn, their rhetorical stance is not simply oppositional, but defensive—they enact the uneasy relation of the subject and his culture—and they can be understood best in relation to such other defensive documents as Wyatt's letters to his son or his formal defense of 1541.

Denial

From the opening lines of these poems, the warm and assured modulation of Wyatt's epistolary voice projects the poise, equanimity, and familiar authority that are the rhetorical markers of cultural entitlement, refiguring the diversity of individual courtier's interests into the common cultural position of moral independence. In rare moments of Stoic pronouncement this independence will be categorically declared: "Then seek no more out of thyself to find / The thing that thou hast sought so long before, / For thou shalt find it sitting in thy mind" (150.97–99). Here Wyatt translates a well-known tag from Persius (1.7): *ne te quaesiveris ultra,* "seek not thyself without." But most of the time such open philosophical proclamation is gratuitous. The very worldliness of the voice—its richness, its calm gravity, its *savoir vivre*—provides a figure for its distance from the world, claiming an independence from the culture that authorizes it. But Wyatt's verse epistles are not ultimately inward or reflective; their defensiveness forecloses any confessional inwardness. Indeed, this voice of inner truth speaks largely in social commentary, establishing its moral privilege in relation to the defects of the world from which it claims to withdraw, measuring its moral strength by the power it repudiates. The rhetoric of moral independence, then, like the rhetoric of patriarchy, is strained—especially when it is most persuasive—and one discovers in the beautifully modulated resonances of Wyatt's verse epistles the abiding anxieties of his position.

In his two letters of advice to his son, I have argued, Thomas Wyatt was writing himself into the part of a father, and in "Mine own John Poyntz," almost certainly written, like the letters, following Wyatt's gentle punishment at Allington for his involvement in the scandal of Anne Boleyn, Wyatt writes himself into the role of the morally privileged outsider and observer. I emphasize Wyatt's writerly fabrication here, the foregrounded production of his voice in "letters," because Wyatt discovered the authentic moral voice of the verse epistles in reading and rewriting the satires of Luigi Alamanni, a republican exile from Medici Florence who found courtly employment (and an audience appreciative of the latest Italian fashion) in the service of Francis I. "Mine own John Poyntz" is a very close translation of Alamanni's tenth satire, published in his *Opere Toscane* in Lyons in 1532, and one way to query the unity and authenticity of Wyatt's poem is to examine its closeness to its source.

Alamanni addresses his poem to his friend Tomasso Sertini from his rural retreat in Provence, deploying a series of rhetorical formulas to explain the reasons for his voluntary exile from the society of king and peers. "I cannot," he reiterates in the first of two long rhetorical series, "distort the truth. . . . I cannot respect those who care only for Venus and Bacchus. . . . I cannot call a cruel man just and strict."[2] Alamanni now lives, he explains, in the obscurity, poverty, and peace of Provence, enjoying a serenity he evokes by deploying another rhetorical series: "I am not in France to suffer insults about my ignorance of wine. . . . I am not in Germany to drink beer." It is precisely the repetitive rhetoricity of Alamanni's verse that Wyatt imitates, reproducing almost line for line the sustained parallelism of Alamanni's two insistent series. To be sure, Wyatt shifts the historical referents in his translation autobiographically, moving the locale from Provence to Kent, changing the addressee from Sertini to his fellow courtier John Poyntz.[3] And he is scrupulous in keeping his English idiomatic, often substituting homely images and proverbial allusions for abstractions. But this English voice is projected through an imitative ventriloquism; Wyatt's "I" defines itself and its "homeward" movement to "Kent and Christendom" by speaking almost to the letter the rhetorical script laid out in the Italian model. Only rarely does Wyatt add, condense, or omit, and the definitive rhetorical movement of the poem is that of its source. This surrender to the iterative rhetoric of his source is functional, palliative, and therapeutic. It is a neutral yielding to another authority. As Wyatt wrote to his son of the need for such sources of rhetorical commonplaces as Seneca and Epictetus: "ye had neede to gathir an hepe of good opinions and to get them perfectly as it were on your fingers ends: Reason not greatly upon the approuing of them, take them as already approved bicaus they wer of honest mens leauings."[4]

The rhetoric to which Wyatt yields here is one of opposition, for the "I" is defined by the courtly deception that "I cannot" practice, by the foreign realms where "I am not." This rhetoric of denial has some of the uncertain dramatic qualities of ritual renunciation, each negative clause a fresh exercise of will that must stay denial from collapsing into submission. But the incremental effect of the tirade, which increasingly realizes the moral psychology of the renouncing "I," depends not simply upon the stone wall of reiterated negation, but upon the continuing refiguration of the terms denied. No act of negation is pure, for denial predicates the thing denied, and the courtly misrepresentations that the "I" repudiates here are displayed in a distinctly allegorical field, above all in the allusions to history and letters that Wyatt domesticates in translating:

> I cannot wrest the law to fill the coffer,
> With innocent blood to feed myself fat,
> And do most hurt where most help I offer.

> I am not he that can allow the state
> Of him Caesar and damn Cato to die,
> That with his death did 'scape out of the gate
> From Caesar's hands, if Livy doth not lie,
> And would not live where liberty was lost,
> So did his heart the common wealth apply.
> I am not he such eloquence to boast
> To make the crow singing as the swan,
> Nor call "the lion" of coward beasts the most
> That cannot take a mouse as the cat can;
> And he that dieth for hunger of the gold,
> Call him Alexander, and say that Pan
> Passeth Apollo in music many fold;
> Praise Sir Thopas for a noble tale
> And scorn the story that the knight told;
> Praise him for counsel that is drunk of ale;
> Grin when he laugheth that beareth all the sway,
> Frown when he frowneth and groan when he is pale,
> On other's lust to hang both night and day.
> (149.34–55)

In renouncing the Henrician court (which had just most kindly and gently rejected him) Wyatt refigures it within an economy of courtly letters that can register the moral order of Chaucer's knight or of Aesop's fables and that can find a place to articulate the interests of the commonwealth against the incursion of Caesar and tyranny. He also refigures the neoclassical authority of his source in a field of national letters. This secular and vernacular cultural authority is surely a part of the corrupt courtly discourse it critiques, but it is important to recognize the positive logic at work in the act of denial. Without it, the denying "I" breaks into inarticulate fear: "I cannot, I. No, no, it will not be!" (76).

The "I" also figures itself into this economy of letters that it speaks, for retreat from the court makes it possible not only "to hunt and hawk" but "in foul weather at my book to sit" (80–81). And the epistle closes by evoking the "home" to which the "I" withdraws as the dwelling place of the Muses:

> I am not now in France to taste the wine . . .
> Nor I am not where Christ is given in prey
> For money, poison, and treason in Rome—
> A common practice used night and day.
> But here I am in Kent and Christendom
> Among the Muses where I read and rhyme,

> Where if thou list, my Poyntz, for to come,
> Thou shalt be judge how I do spend my time.
>   (149.89, 97–103)

At this very moment when the rhetoric of the poem shifts from denial into assertion, when Wyatt is specifying the concrete locus of his retreat, the place
where he *is*, his language mystifies the geography, rewriting the proverbial
"Kent or Christendom" (Kent was an early holdout against the Anglo-Saxon
conversion while paradoxically the spiritual center of England in Canterbury)
to make his father's country place into a spiritual home informed by Christian revelation and mediated by the independent moral understanding of
human letters.

The assertion is an appealing one, but its idealizing rhetoric is fragile.
The poem ends with an invitation. John Poyntz, the courtier whose questions about why Wyatt was leaving the court initiated this long answer, is
invited to join Wyatt in rural retreat. The invitation is innocent enough,
and the "I" is confident enough to offer the invitation. But the invitation
opens up again the uneasy rhetorical balance of the poem, between the "I"
and the court he denies, between the "I" and the rhetoric into which he has
inserted himself. Must the literary economy of the muses be validated by
the social and political economy of the court? Does "I" depend upon the ap-
probation of "thou"? Has Wyatt invited Poyntz to serve as the very kind of
courtly judge that the imaginary landscape of Kent and Christendom has
been erected to censor out?

The invitation to Poyntz to "judge how I do spend my time" circles the
poem uneasily back to its origins in Wyatt's rustication from court in the
bloody spring of 1536. The autobiographical rewriting that Wyatt used to
appropriate Alamanni's rhetoric insists tellingly on the continuing influence
of the court; it escapes the blind discipline of rhetorical imitation. Wyatt has
claimed all along that his own independent moral judgment is what "makes"
him withdraw homeward, but this claim overlaps with the suggestion that it
has been royal judgment that "makes" him stay there. He enjoys the "news"
(novelties) of this unfamiliar life in the country,

> But of these news I feel nor weal nor woe
> Since that a clog doth hang yet at my heel,
> No force for that, for it is ordered so
> That I may leap both hedge and dike full well.
>   (149.80–89)

Alamanni spends his time in Provence of his own free will ("volontier dimoro"). But the liberty Wyatt enjoys is licensed by the gentlemanly understanding of the royal order: he is "free" to ride and hunt as long as he stays at home. The alternative moral order of the denying "I" is a defensive one. In the country, indeed in the therapeutic rhetoric of retreat, the speaker is "to will and lust learning to set a law"—a self-discipline that is set in uneasy complicity with the law that has imposed this rustication, for it was precisely this "will and lust" ("rage," "unthriftness," and "foly" were the self-castigating phrases the repentant Wyatt had used in the letter to his son[5]) that the law of the court had condemned in him. In its defensiveness, then, the denying "I" betrays its insecurity, and its independent rhetoric is subject to unconscious collapse.

What does it mean, for example, to substitute Cato for Brutus as a figure of resistance?

> I am not he that can allow the state
> Of him Caesar and damn Cato to die,
> That with his death did 'scape out of the gate
> From Caesar's hands, if Livy doth not lie,
> And would not live where liberty was lost,
> So did his heart the common wealth apply.
>
> (149.37–42)

Suppressing the treasonous thought of tyrannicide is fair enough, and Cato is perhaps a virtuous martyr. But Wyatt's speaker would *not* have Cato die, and his syntax conjoins Cato's death (by whose hand is not mentioned) to his own countenancing of Caesar's magnificence; the speaker refers the cause of Cato's death not to suicide but to the complicity of the "I." Cato's suicide thus contaminates the proud resistance of the speaking subject's denial, subliminally suggesting suicide too as a means of escape from "Caesar's hands" and perhaps from the "clog." And why does Wyatt introduce suspicions against the source [6] from which he has drawn his rewriting of Alamanni: "if Livy doth not lie"? Is this another form of denial? Is Cato's suicide too not credible? Unthinkable? This passing "if," also threatens the speaker's investment in the moral order of letters, for if Livy lies, why not Chaucer, why not Aesop, and so why not the Wyatt of the Kentish muses?

I do not wish to suggest that Wyatt's poem is one of submission or of despair, and I believe that it would be equally foolish to suggest that Wyatt's poem sets up in Kent and Christendom a stable alternative to the courtly world he seeks to escape. There is no escape from the world, for it is present in the very language one deploys to shut it out. Stoic withdrawal from the corruption outside to an inner peace is illusory. The outside will return irrepressibly in the speaker's very mode of discourse just as Poyntz, the "absent" addressee, is invited to visit the place of origin of the poem of which he is already rhetorically a part. But it is not foolish to suggest that the rhetorical staging of denial, entitlement, and insecurity as they play through the voice of the speaker provides a cultural avenue for the always changing articulation of the subject. The shifting engagement of the speaking subject with the rhetoric producing his voice is not simply a Manichaean crisis of self-creation and self cancellation, but a literary re-creation of the lifelong process of the subject in what Anthony Giddens has called "continuous structuration,"[7] the necessary, confused, shifting engagement of the speaking subject in a discourse that neither guarantees wholeness or withholds it, that produces him as he produces it.

Disjunction

Another staging of the speaking subject, and perhaps an even less reassuring one, can be found in "My mother's maids." In this poem, the speaker tells a familiar story, the tale of the country mouse and the town mouse. The rhetorical depth of the poem is found in the ways the story is engaged with the speaker who produces it in the larger frame of the verse epistle. The story is followed by a lengthy moral commentary addressed by the speaker to his friend John Poyntz and urging him not to look "out of himself" to find happiness, "For thou shalt find it sitting in thy mind" (150.97–99). Like "Mine own John Poyntz," this poem asserts a voice of moral independence. But it is a voice that is opened up by the rhetorical relation of tale, voice, and commentary. The two parts of the poem are formally separated, the courtly milieu of Wyatt and Poyntz suspended until the second half. And the deferral is suspicious. As the speaker's commentary unfolds, as he speaks his "own" situation, a drama emerges from his rhetorical production that complicates the fable with which the poem began. It is at this very moment of formal authorial control that the rhetoric of the poem becomes most disruptive. And this rhetorical disjunction of tale and commentary is perhaps emblematic of the many other kinds of cultural disjunction that the poem both masks and solicits.

The poem takes as its point of origin a memory of childhood, a tale told in the company of ladies-in-waiting ("maids" in our usage suggests too menial a service) to the speaker's mother in the milk-fed years before the boy of the Tudor establishment (usually at six or seven) was removed from the domestic precincts of the maternal household and inserted into the serial institutions that related men to men: tutelage, school, service in the household of a magnate, university, inns of court, military service, courtly appointments, commissions of the peace, embassies, wardships. The poem begins, not by invoking the name of the speaker's male correspondent—John Poyntz is not addressed until the middle of the poem—but with a clear evocation of the distaff side: "My mother's maids when they did sew and spin, / They sang sometime a song of the field mouse" (150.1–2).

I emphasize these opening lines—not unfairly I think—because they return the tale told by the sophisticated male speaker so unequivocally to the days before his enfranchisement as a gentleman of the court. The story of the country mouse and the city mouse that follows is one familiar from Aesop and from adaptations by Horace and Henryson—among many others. But Wyatt distinctly and factitiously dislocates the story from its classical guarantee and recalls its origin as a *chanson de toile* back in the distantly recalled scene of women at needlework. In part this domestic setting, like "Kent and Christendom," signals a moral retreat from court, here found in the imaginary safety of that briefly imagined scene of women's work and recreation. In part it also betrays a momentary longing to return to the imaginary security of childhood after the disappointments of a busy life. If it has no other remarkable quality, the first line of this poem is the only surviving instance of Thomas Wyatt even mentioning his mother—mothers are generally written out of the ideological family of the Tudor gentleman. The moralizing commentary, on the other hand, is distinctly addressed by a comfortable man of experience to a fellow man about "men": "Alas, my Poyntz, how men do seek the best, / And find the worst, by error as they stray" (150.70–71). The speaker appropriates the fable, of course, making it his own in rehearsing it, but its putative origin in the distant maternal past, invoked only momentarily at the start, is worth bearing in mind, particularly as the rhetoric of the poem breaks down and the speaker becomes more vulnerable.

The tale that the speaking subject produces here thus becomes at first an example of mastery, for the remembered fable of the ladies-in-waiting is reinvested in its presentation with a confident superiority that belongs to the male subject as the speaker attempts to secure it. Indeed, in the telling of the story, the male voice of the speaker at times patronizes the "homely" wives' tale and the two female mice who are its victims. The tale stands out from its analogues in being one of female victimization. As Rebholz has said of Wyatt's rendition of the fable:

In all known versions before Wyatt's, the fable begins with the town mouse visiting the country mouse, voicing the first attack on country life and the first praise of life in town, and inviting the country mouse to visit. Wyatt has the country mouse attack country life, praise city life, and choose to visit the city mouse who greets her in a state of mental anxiety. Likewise, in all but Wyatt's version, the fable ends with the country mouse finally escaping back to the country—whether it be from butler, dog, cat, or some undefined threat. Wyatt's country mouse does not escape the cat and may possibly be killed by it. (446)

I should add that the naiveté, greed, jealousy, and pride of the victim are inscribed confidently along the lines of gender. And as the speaker produces this tale of victimization, sympathy for the victim and dread for the predator are muted by his superior, ironic critique of the hapless country mouse, making her desire to "reign in wealth" the cause of her capture. For the two "sisters" are clearly Chaucerian gossips who enjoy a good meal and all the perquisites of the wasteful city table; their consciousness, indeed, seems to express itself largely in terms of what they eat and drink: "she feasted her that joy it was to tell / The fare they had" (45–46). The city mouse, moreover, is a type of womanish timidity "of every noise . . . aghast" (39), and the country mouse is a shrew who resents her difficult life, envies her sister (mainly for her well-stocked larder), and would "keep herself in health / To live a lady while her life doth last" (34–35). In the country mouse's great moment of danger, the speaker even toys with the rhetorical ploy of Continental xenophobia, suggesting that the country mouse was more frightened even than the cowardly French ("In France / Was never mouse so feared" [54–55]), and here, as in "Mine own John Poyntz," the device is perhaps as defensive as it is proud.

Indeed, all of this gentle (gentlemanly?) irony has the effect of attempting to distance the speaker defensively from the foolish victims of his tale. There even seems a narrative logic at work; his moralizing intervention in the tale coincides with the capture of the unwitting mouse:

> At the threshold her silly foot did trip,
> And ere she might recover it again
> The traitor cat had caught her by the hip
> And made her there against her will remain,
> That had forgotten her poor surety and rest
> For seeming wealth wherein she thought to reign.
> Alas, my Poyntz, how men do seek the best
> And find the worst by error as they stray!
>
> (150.64–71)

The speaker, like the cat, enjoys having the poor mouse in his grasp. For as the story is left in suspense, with the fate of the country sister unknown, the speaker cuts it off and points an easy moral, adorning the homely tale with a Stoic philosophical authority. But as he moralizes the story, he introduces now for the first time his own circumstances in the address to John Poyntz, and the speaker's self-possession and his calm and confident appropriation of his material begin to break down.

One way of recognizing this disintegration is simply to look at the terms of address. For Poyntz, finally named as the addressee here, is not the only one to whom the speaker's words are directed. The pronouns of address alternate between a personal "thou" (Poyntz) and a generalized plural "ye all."[8] At times this shift is imperceptible, and I should not remark on it at all if it were not symptomatic of the larger and more debilitating disjunctions that are at work here. The address to "thou" tends to be more confident, advisory, and understanding:

> Live in delight even as thy lust would
> And thou shalt find, when lust doth most thee please,
> It irketh straight and by itself doth fade . . .
> . . . Thyself content with that is thee assigned
> And use it well that is to thee allotted.
> Then seek no more out of thyself to find
> The thing that thou hast sought so long before,
> For thou shalt find it sitting in thy mind.
>   (150.81–83, 95–99)

In using "thou," the speaker is addressing his friend Poyntz personally. Although he may speak critically, he is never vituperative; he is encouraging rather than scolding or condemning. The "you," on the other hand, is adversarial, corrupt, an "other" that the speaker seeks to exclude: "Mad, if ye list to continue your sore,/Let present pass and gape on time to come/And deep yourself in travail more and more" (100–2).[9] Ultimately, the "you" disintegrates into a damning "they," as the speaker turns from addressing Poyntz to invoking a parting curse against those courtly fools that he renounces:

> Henceforth, my Poyntz, this shall be all and sum.
> These wretched fools shall have naught else of me.
> But to the great God and to his high doom
> None other pain pray I for them to be
> But when the rage doth lead them from the right,
> That looking backward, Virtue they may see

> Even as she is, so goodly fair and bright.
> And whilst they clasp their lusts in arms across,
> Grant them, good Lord, as thou mayst of thy might,
> To fret inward for losing such a loss.
>
> (150.103–12)

In these final lines the speaker's critique of courtly ambition slides into defensiveness. He does not simply celebrate his stoic withdrawal from the corruption of society, or call for his friend Poyntz to join him in the moral freedom of retreat, but seeks to vindicate himself through the ultimate humiliation of the "wretched fools." His language here loses its patience, its ability to suffer abuses with an unflagging sense of righteousness; the tone takes on more than a trace of injured merit.

Like Wyatt's "Stand whoso list," this poem ends in imagining the pained last moment of conscience in the corrupt and powerful. And like that poem, it rearranges the picture of that last moment that it had found in its Latin subtext, which is, in effect, another "other" that he is using to define himself against. In this final address to the "good Lord," Wyatt takes on the stance of a righteous and scorned prophet, but his indignant Christian imprecation is a translation of some celebrated lines from Persius's third satire (35–38): "Great father of the gods! Be it thy will to punish cruel tyrants whose souls have been stirred by the burning poison of deadly lust in no other way but this—that they may look on virtue, and waste away because they have lost her" (my translation). Wyatt enhances the idealized Virtue ("so goodly fair and bright"); he christianizes Jove; he suppresses "cruel tyrants," generalizing to "they," but he makes concrete the lines about lust, imagining lust (*dira libido*) in the erotic image of an embrace with a woman: "and whilst they clasp their lusts in arms across." It is from that sensual embrace that the corrupt "they" are to experience the *inward* pain (conscience is again Wyatt's emphasis) of their error.

I should not wish to argue that Wyatt refers here exclusively or even consciously to the "tyrant" whose title he has suppressed in translation. But I believe that there is no reasonable way to argue that such lines, especially given the dynastic reshuffling of 1536 (or for that matter again of 1541), does not at least implicate the king at the level of subliminal allegory, for his second divorce (from Anne) and betrothal (to Jane Seymour following hard upon Anne's execution) had made him even in the most sympathetic minds a signifier easily receptive to figuring the image of unbridled erotic desire. Indeed, the poem here toys with this notion, and this discursive risk is part of the pleasure of the translation, writing out the title of the king ("cruel tyrants") and simultaneously writing the figure of the king into the poem through the personified embrace.

The speaker of this poem moves from being philosophical to being defensive and vindictive. His stoic response to adversity seems all too patently to have originated in a personal and deeply ingrained sense of failure, betrayal, and disappointment. Indeed, the poem is suspended dramatically, not from the remembered story that it claims as its rhetorical origin, but from this moment of renunciation: "these wretched fools shall have no more of me." And as one learns more of this speaker, it is impossible to take the opening story of the country mouse and the city mouse on his terms. He has gone out of his way to "blame" the country mouse. As Rebholz comments: "it is the country mouse who freely but mistakenly chooses the life of material wealth and pleasure which the town mouse, from experience, knows is a source of anxiety. And the country mouse is trapped in, perhaps even destroyed by, the consequences of her choice, since—unlike escape into the country from city or court—there is no easy escape from anxiety of mind or heart" (446). There is no figure in the fable who escapes to a guaranteed realm of "conscience." The fable would otherwise imply that the quiet life, apart from the corruption of civilization, is a means of assuring inner peace. And there is no representation in the fable itself of inner peace won and enjoyed. For has not the speaker in exposing himself as the escaped victim of the "wretched fools" of the court finally identified himself in part with the canny (and cowardly) town mouse? The towny sister mouse who escapes does so, after all, not through moral withdrawal but through the insider's knowledge of a fast way out: "she knew whither to go." So does the speaker.

I should suggest, then, that the initial withdrawal of the poem into the feminized rhetorical space of the Aesopian fable is a suspect one, and that the poem, in "mastering" the Aesopian text of the fable, also corrupts it, suggesting, contrary to the Aesopian moral, that the only "moral" escape from the world that provides one's identity is an easy and temporary "rhetorical" one. The speaker's own withdrawal, his "rhetorical" renunciation of the court and his parting curse are just that easy way out; he does not go back with the country mouse to her rural retreat to celebrate the virtues of retirement nor does he lament its loss; the celebration of the inward life of the independent mind that the story promises is deflected, and it disintegrates into a bitter curse against the speaker's oppressors, moving from a critique of the silly mouse's gluttony to a critique of courtly greed, ambition, and lust. Indeed, one must wonder if the inward "fretting" and regret that the speaker expresses in this final curse are not directed against himself.

The suppressed "tyrant" of the closing lines of the commentary and the deferred "teller" of the tale—for it is the speaker's tale, after all, not that of "his mothers' maids"—are also identified with one another in the subliminal figurative logic of the poem. The confident voice that can blame "them" for his corrupt world—this is the aggressive voice that coincides with the cat— cannot separate himself from "them" as easily as he would wish after his initial rhetorical pounce. Let us consider again the transitional lines from tale to commentary in fuller context:

> Alas, my Poyntz, how men do seek the best
> And find the worst by error as they stray!
> And no marvel, when sight is so oppressed,
> And blind the guide, anon, out of the way
> Goeth guide and all in seeking quiet life.
> (150.70–74)

The other that he attacks so virulently is something sensed within himself. Like the speaker in "Mine own John Poyntz," he too is "to will and lust learning to set a law." As Stephen Greenblatt has commented in *Renaissance Self-Fashioning*: "The satirist claims to have a *center* in his life from which he speaks with secure assurance, but he pays for this claim in the coldness that lurks beneath the surface energy, the stiffening that seems to preclude the possibility of full emotional life. Sexuality has diminished to nothing: the satirist defines himself by his attack on sexual viciousness in the court and his stoic dismissal of the pursuit of pleasure." His renunciation of the court is a kind of repression; the "they" embracing their "lusts in arms across," seeing Virtue in retrospect, "so goodly fair and bright," stand in part for the speaker himself. The blind guide whom the speaker believes erring men to follow is, after all, a prominent figure in the spare mythography of Wyatt's erotic psychology. Perhaps the regret, the backward look, the loss of virtue is experienced, not only by the "they" of the poem, but by the speaker who erects this rhetoric to exclude "them"? Is not their regret his as well?

In his letter to his son, Wyatt had indeed dwelt upon just such a "repining":

No doubt in any thing you doo, if you axe your self or examine the thing for yourself afore you doo it, you shal find, if it be euill, a repining against it. My son, for our lords love, kepe wel that repining: suffer it not to be darkid and corrupted by noughty example, as tho any thing were excusable to you becaus other men doo the same. That same repining, if it did punisch as he doth iuge, wer no such iusticer. And, of truth, so doth it punisch, but not so apparantly. Here how we think it no smal grefe of a consciens that condemnith it self, but be wel asurid aftir this life it is a continual gnawing.[10]

Conscience—the inward court of Wyatt's ethics—provides a means of trial both in the control of the moral agent and also outside his control, since it continues in time and can judge memory; it is both a court of moral action and a court that can perpetually mete out punishment for his lapses ex post facto, stricter even than divine judgment. He must use his conscience to make his own moral choices, and, even if he makes an error, conscience will sit in judgment against him. In this poem, too, the moral life is tried through inward fretting. And the neat boundaries that the speaker would erect between his own inner incorruptibility and the renunciation of the corrupt outside break down more along the ambiguous lines suggested in the letter.

The gendered narrative rhetoric that scripts victimization as female is a defensive mode here as it is in much of Wyatt's work, and I leave this poem open to speculation by inviting consideration of another story that begins with a scene of women's work:

> She sat and sewed that hath done me the wrong
> Whereof I plain and have done many a day,
> And whilst she heard my plaint in piteous song
> Wished my heart the sampler as it lay.
> The blind master whom I have served so long,
> Grudging to hear that he did hear her say,
> Made her own weapon do her finger bleed
> To feel if pricking were so good indeed.
>
> (41)

Like "My mother's maids," and like its companion poem on the same theme, "Who hath heard of such cruelty before" (53), this *strambotto* plays on the tensions between the discourses of women and men. Here, the rapacious wit of the speaker refigures the needle, inscribing a language of rejection and injury across the imagined body of the lover in the lady's embroidered sampler, turning the needle into an intellectual vehicle of male penetration, possessing her in a pornographic pun, finding vengeance for her coldness in his own cold sexual innuendo. "My mother's maids" ironically turns a childhood tale into a cynical courtly allegory, rejecting the simple earnestness of the Aesopian moral because, like the "maids" from whom Wyatt first heard the tale, it inscribes an unempowered and vulnerable world. As in "She sat and sewed," this is defensive, compensatory, reactionary rhetoric indeed, and there is a lingering hollowness in its pride. Perhaps one reason its speaker returns to the childhood memory of women at needlework is that he identifies too strongly with his imagined fear of their disenfranchisement and vulnerability. He is defending himself against identification with the spineless but clever town sister. Through this evasive and cynical rescripting he is also perhaps defending himself as a "man" against the boy who once believed in the imagined wholeness, purity, and simplicity of the impossibly past maternal world that the speaker now momentarily projects in introducing his tale.

Impersonations

Just as "My mother's maids" exposes the moral fragility of the fable, "A spending hand" exposes another Tudor cultural authority, the proverb, an ideological function that stands in place of the individual human subjects who speak it. The rhetorical commonplace, we have seen in Wyatt's first letter to his son, is a source or, to use the rhetorical term suggested by its etymology, a topos or "place" of moral security, an impersonal repository of wisdom from the treasury of letters: "Reason not greatly upon the approving of them, take them as already approved bicaus they wer of honest mens leauings."[11] The commonplace, then, is theoretically an untroubled position for the speaking subject to occupy. In the opening lines of "A spending hand," however, the commonplace becomes the site for some disruptive, unsettling contradiction among images, speakers, and intentions, and between the terms of address. The speaker ironically quotes proverbs that graphically deprecate waste and rapid, unpurposeful movement as examples of lasting cultural authority:

> "A spending hand that always poureth out
> Hath need to have a bringer in as fast";
> And "On that stone that still doth turn about
> There groweth no moss"—these proverbs yet do last.
> Reason hath set them in so sure a place
> That length of years their force can never waste.
>   (151.1–6)

This play between permanence and loss initiates the unruly rhetorical and logical movement of the poem. The speaker addresses a fellow courtier, Sir Francis Brian, who, he claims, has a knowledge of the lasting moral authority that writings like proverbs possess, advising him, cynically, that given such sententious wisdom, the pursuit of right action in courtly service is a frantic waste of motion:

When I remember this and eke the case
Wherin thou stands, I thought forthwith to write,
Brian, to thee, who knows how great a grace
In writing is to counsel man the right.
To thee therefore, that trots still up and down
And never rests, but running day and night
From realm to realm, from city, street and town,
Why dost thou wear thy body to the bones
And mightst at home sleep in thy bed of down
And drink good ale so nappy for the nonce,
Feed thyself fat and heap up pound by pound?
                                        (151.7–17)

The speaker, then, has turned the proverbs against commonplace pieties: the "rolling stone" is transformed from the listless wanderer to the devoted and hardworking civil servant posted from city to city on the king's service. The "spending hand" is not luxurious self-indulgence but the normal high expense of maintaining the (always extravagant) life appropriate to one's station. The place of proverbs, then, is not so sure as the speaker opaquely suggests, for it is not a geographical place or a place on the body, but a rhetorical topos, and "reason" can pervert as well as preserve what is written to "counsel men the right." Writing can serve the cynical speaker as well as the supposedly righteous Brian. "The right" is whatever one calls it. In the words of "Mine own John Poyntz," this kind of discourse is to "praise Sir Tophas for a noble tale, / And scorn the story that the knight told" (149.50–51). In such a discourse the waste or expense that the proverb deprecates is exposed as a universal condition of exchange. Speech here does not necessarily mean communication; it is a rolling stone.

This kind of slippage, of course, is built into the disturbing dialectical structure of the poem, for the speaker, possessing all the aesthetic qualities of the speakers of Wyatt's other satires—the blunt honesty, the manly directness—is clearly "voicing" the arguments of the morally degenerate and unthinkingly powerful men that this same persuasive gentlemanly "voice" teaches us to reject in the other verse epistles. Ironically, of all three verse epistles, this is the one that most explicitly advertises its generic status as a "letter" with a clearly designated signator and addressee: "I thought forthwith to write, / Brian, to thee, who knows how great a grace / In writing is to counsel men the right" (8–10). But the "letter" is manifestly (and impossibly) a dialogue, and the terms of address of the two genres seem uncomfortably skewed. If this is a letter, what is Brian's "voice" doing in it? If this is a dialogue—like one of its models, the dialogue of Tiresias and Ulysses in Horace's Satire 2.5—then why is it addressed as a written epistle to Brian?

Some have argued that the confusion in the terms of address extends beyond the inversion of the Wyatt persona to topical play on the historical character of Sir Francis Brian. According to Stephen Greenblatt, the choice of Brian as the spokesman for "the values of goodliness and an honest name" indicates Wyatt's explicit awareness of the way his culture suppressed or "forgot" the corruption not just of individual courtiers but of the entire courtly system:

> These are the very last things the historical Francis Brian possessed or represented: wit, bravery, and the ability to survive, yes, but not an honest name. . . . His was a career of conniving, betrayal, politic marriage, sycophancy, and pandering. Though Wyatt's poem seems quite deliberately to avoid turning its satire against Brian, more than one of the vices it catalogues bear an uncanny resemblance to well-known incidents in Brian's life. There is no explicit internal evidence for an ironic reversal, an exposure of his unscrupulous boon companion as a mock honest man (just as the speaker had pretended to be a mock corrupt man), but some such thought must at least have crossed Wyatt's mind.[12]

Brian had married a wealthy widow, Lady Fortescue, in 1517; his nickname at court—a reflection of his racy style—was the "vicar of hell." He was also known as a collector of proverbs and as a poet, and his poems are perhaps among those by uncertain authors in Tottel.[13] But Wyatt, too, was well known for his interest in proverbial sayings and for his use of them, and the abiding cultural interest of the complex rhetorical inversions of the poem lies in its scrutiny of the embedded cultural problem of mistaken identity or impersonation. Wyatt impersonates Brian in writing Brian a letter; the use of proverbs, too, is an impersonation of authority; and it is precisely the question of how an individual human subject can be made to say words that are not his that is put at risk here. We do not hear Brian's voice, nor do we hear Wyatt's; we read a poem in which their names have been attached to the words of a dialogue that "they" did not write. The "author" of this poem recedes into his words.

The simple inversion of persona is not really the issue, for there would be a passing, ironic clarity in inversion, and Greenblatt is quite right in saying that "Wyatt's poem seems quite deliberately to avoid turning its satire against Brian."[14] What, then, are the implications of Greenblatt's declaration that such a thought must "at least have crossed Wyatt's mind"? The danger that this poem broaches is the unspeakable possibility that virtue and vice speak the same language and understand one another like gentlemen. The Brian character, after all, does not tell the Wyatt character to shove off. He takes it in good spirit. "Laughest thou at me" asks Wyatt, and "Brian" replies, "No, not at thee, but at thy thrifty jest" (79–80). "It is but love," the voice of Wyatt had said before of a romantic scruple against marriage for money, "turn it to a laughter" (72). Indeed, from the start of the poem, some of the most ideologically compelling locutions of the Wyatt voice are shared by his interlocutor, for both voices linger over satiric images of pouring out, of excrement, of consumption, of feeding, rotting, and bestiality. If the Wyatt persona invites his friend to live the "good life," sleeping in his bed of down and drinking "good ale so nappy for the nonse," feeding himself "fat" and heaping up "pound by pound" (15–17), the indignant retort of the virtuous Brian performs a similar alimentary reduction. He refuses,

> For swine so groins
> In sty and chaw the turds moulded on the ground,
> And drivel on pearls, the head still in the manger.
> Then of the harp the ass do hear the sound.
> So sacks of dirt be filled up in the cloister,
> That serves for less than do these fatted swine.
> Tho I seem lean and dry without moisture,
> Yet will I serve my prince, my lord and thine,
> And let them live to fede the paunch that list
> So I may feed to live, both me and mine.
>
> (151.18–27)

Easy moral distinctions break down in the spillage of scatological rhetoric. The moral voice of Brian takes its strength by descending with a satiric fascination and relish into the life of the lower body; the potential shrillness of his moralistic voice is mitigated by the pornographic repugnance and attraction of the images he summons. Brian launches a ringing acclamation for the service of the king, but the telltale rhyme words of the terza rima drag the good name of that monarch—"my lord and thine"—and the speaker himself back into the alimentary process "So I may feed to live, both me and mine." What the speakers agree on, after all, is that one can equate some human activities (as opposed to others) with "waste." To the Brian voice, service to the status quo of king and country is *de rigeur,* while to look for mere personal profit or ease is a form of "chawing turds." To the Wyatt voice, eating, sleeping, or enjoying the inheritance of a widow with a "rivelled skin, a stinking breath, . . . a toothless mouth" (61–62) are all moments to be enjoyed for the profit. The conflict between the two speakers seems to ask what is waste and what is profit and to blur the answer. After all, to the one mere self-profit is "waste"; to the other, self-indulgent "waste" is the best kind of profit: "Feed theyself fat and heap up pound by pound, p. 158." Indeed, the "Wyatt" speaker states at one point,

> See thou when there thy gain may be the more.
> Stay him by the arm where so he walk or go.
> Be near alway, and if he cough too sore,
> When he hath spit, tread out and please him so.
>   (151.52–55)

To "Brian," only animals live on their own waste; to "Wyatt", human waste signals the occasion for profit: dirt is gold. It is men like Brian, in his view, who act like beasts—not because they live in filth, but because they have been reduced to a bestial docility: as a dutiful ambassador Brian "trots still up and down."

Wyatt's words here describing the taxing routine of an ambassador on the road, are, as commentaries have often noted, very close to words that Wyatt also used to describe his own diligent service to the king in his "declaration of his innocence" to the council in 1541: "I, as God iudge me, lyke as I was contynually imagininge and cumpassinge what waye I myght do beste seruice: so restede I not day nor nyght to hunte owte for knowledge of those thynges; I trottēd contynually vp and downe that helle through heate and stinke from Councelloure to Embassator, from one frende to an other, but the thynges then were ether so secretly handlede or yett not in couerture that I with all myne acquayntance . . . could gett any knowledge."[15] The importance of the echo—whichever of the texts is prior, poem or declaration—is not that it fixes the date of the poem but that it identifies Wyatt with the character he has given Brian in "A spending hand," continuing, as it were, the overlapping rhetoric of "Wyatt" and "Brian" and confirming the complex confusions of identity that the poem initiates. The "place" of proverbs in the poem also recalls Wyatt's own engagement with problems of identity and impersonation.

For the use and abuse of proverbs to inscribe upon a speaking subject a cultural authority from outside of "himself" indeed caught up with Wyatt during this last imprisonment in 1541. Among the charges that Bonner levelled against him was that he had slandered the king with a vulgar commonplace: "By goddes bludde, ye shall see the kinge our maister cast out at the carts tail, and if he soo be serued, by godds body, he is well serued."[16] Wyatt's formal "defense," an apologetic oration prepared for delivery at his trial (he was released before trial), painstakingly looks into the working of proverbs. Wyatt freely admits that his language is colloquial, even that he enjoys an occasional blasphemy. But his accusers have merely colored language attributed to him with manly oaths to make it seem plausible: "But bycawse I am wonte some tyme to rappe owte an othe in an erneste tawlke, looke how craftylie theie have put in an othe to the matter to mayke the matter seem myne; and bycawse theie have garded an nowghtie garmente of thers with on of my nawghttie gardes theie wyll swere and face me downe that that was my garment. But bringe me my garment as yt was."[17] Wyatt goes on to contend that although he may have said something similar to what his accusers have attributed to him, the context and the precise wording must be considered:

yt is a smale thynge in the alteringe of one syllable ether with penne or worde that may mayk in the conceavinge of the truthe myche matter or error. For in thys thynge "I fere" or "I truste" semethe but one smale syllabel chaynged, and yet it makethe a great dyfferaunce, and may be of an herer wronge conceaved and worse reported, and yet worste of all altered by an examyner. Agayne "fall owte," "caste owt," or "lefte owte" makethe dyfferaunce, yea and the setting of the wordes one in an others place may mayke great dyfferaunce, tho the wordes were al one—as "a myll horse" and a "horse myll."[18]

The narrow point that is at issue here is the meaning of the proverb, "I am left out at the cartes ass." It suggests that whatever is loaded onto a cart hastily, loosely, negligently, will slip unsecured out of the back of the cart and be lost. Wyatt explains that in describing the negotiation between the two warring monarchs, Francis and Charles, more concerned with one another than with Henry, he might well have said something like, "I fere for all these mens fayer promyses the kinge shalbe lefte owte of the cartes ars" and thus "lament that many good occasions had bene lett slyppe of concludinge with one of their princes."[19] Wyatt's accusers he claims, have taken the remark out of context—they have not rendered his "garment" whole—and they have made their prevarication plausible by impersonating Wyatt's voice.

I linger over this segment from Wyatt's defense, then, not merely because of the verbal parallels to "A spending hand," but because these two moments from Wyatt's life, poem and defense, are so deeply engaged with the larger cultural problems of identity and impersonation. The poem, like Wyatt's defense, exposes the very kinds of discursive mechanisms like the proverb that men and women use to give themselves authority, to project their identity before others. As Wyatt's metaphor suggests, they are rhetorical "garments" that one puts on, and the problem of personal identity extends beyond the self: in the exchange between Wyatt and Brian are exposed many of the ideological soft spots in the social tissue initiated by this new generation of English "governors." Of particular moment, I believe, are the ways in which the discourses of class and economy seem to put one another at risk.

For much of the poem, both Wyatt and Brian attempt to deflect the impact of their satire away from themselves and their social peers. Brian, for example, brings in the easy image of the lazy monk from estates satire (a safe topic in the late 1530s, when monasteries reverted to the crown and passed, one by one, to courtiers, Wyatt among them, as gifts for services rendered). Some of Wyatt's allusions to profitmaking are similarly class-bound and thus defensive. His "rule" about lending, for example, is clearly aimed at distinguishing the ethics of the so-called landed classes from those of the City and its merchants:

> Lend in no wise, for fear that thou do want,
> Unless it be as to a dog a cheese;
> By which return be sure to win a cant
> Of half at least—it is not good to leese.
> Learn at Kitson, that in a long white coat
> From under the stall without land or fees
> Hath lept into the shop; who knoweth by rote
> This rule that I have told thee herebefore.
>   (151.43–50)

Wyatt ironically rails against the aristocratic largesse of spending and lending and borrowing to meet expenses—this is after all a means of proving power in an economy of display and expenditure. And the bourgeois ethics of saving, striving, and upward mobility are caricatured as meanness in Kitson, who was apparently notorious as a usurer; and the terms, typically, are from the physiology of waste: cheese was supposed to have been an emetic for dogs.[18] The portrait of the estate-snatcher is likewise urban and middle class—it is also very close to its Horatian source. But curiously, as the abuses that the Wyatt speaker ironically advocates become more and more depraved and repugnant, his language and field of reference come closer and closer to the culture of the court, above all in the allusions to love and marriage:

> Thy niece, thy cousin, thy sister, or thy daughter,
> If she be fair, if handsome be her middle,
> If thy better hath her love besought her,

> Advance his cause and he shall help thy need.
> It is but love. Turn it to a laughter.
> But ware, I say, so gold thee help and speed
> That in this case thou be not so unwise
> As Pandar was in such a like deed;
> For he, the fool, of conscience was so nice
> That he no gain would have for all his pain.
> Be next thyself, for friendship bears no prize.
> (151.68–78)

With these lines, the speaker enters dangerously into the area where the ideology of romantic love intersects the economy of dynastic wealth, where the interests of father, brother, or guardian are written onto the body of sister, wife, and ward. The allusion to Chaucer's *Troilus and Cresseide* may perhaps be intended merely to bring out the name of Pandar but it also suggests that the whole world of courtly love synonymous with that poem may not be mediated by the concerns of honor—Wyatt reduces the term to conscience—but by self-interest. The self-knowledge that the speaker of "My mother's maids" had striven for ("Then seek no more out of thyself to find / The thing that thou hast sought so long before, / For thou shalt feel in sitting in thy mind" 150.98–100) has relapsed into mere monetary self-interest: "Be next thyself." The lofty stoic moralism of Persius (*nec te quaesiveris ultra* [Satire 1.7]) has fallen into the comic flippancy of Terence: *proximius sum egomet mihi* (*Andria*, 4.1.12).

Chapter Four

Revising the Script

In 1524, Henry Wyatt received a license to found a chantry, to be called "Sir Henry Wyatt's chantry," in the old chapel of Saint Mary in Melton Church near Gravesend, Kent, not far from Allington Castle. Ten chaplains were to be resident in the chantry, saying cycles of masses daily for the repose of the souls of Henry Wyatt and his heirs forever. This was to be a foundation established in perpetuity, for the glory of God and for the spiritual ease of its founder. Its constitution is spelled out according to the letter of the law, with a clear title to the chantry properties and a clear right to establishment as a body corporate with common seal.[1] This was a year of moment for the Wyatt family: Thomas Wyatt would appear to have become securely established in the royal household as clerk of the jewel house; his father was at the peak of his career as treasurer of the chamber. It was an appropriate time, then, for the family to cap their achievements with the establishment of a chantry, a traditional status marker among the elite—aristocratic and mercantile alike—signalling their arrival in this world by arranging to have prayers said for their translation to the next. Elite culture in early Henrician England was devout to the last scruple of social observance, and no courtier was more scrupulous in his observance than the king himself: he was a distinctly superstitious man, and he prided himself on his theological expertise.

Daily mass was a constant feature of life at court in England as in all the states of Europe—or of Christendom—to use the term (something like "the West") they found most useful for describing their loose sense of international community, and politics was inseparable from religion. And I mean inseparable literally because the church was not simply "established" by a prior state but enmeshed from the start in all the many systems of authority at work in early modern England. The court, like all other lay institutions—the guildhalls of the rich city merchants, for example—was never independent of the life of the church, for the church was everywhere, from the ringing of bells to tell the daily hours to the ecclesiastical calendar that marked the dates and seasons of the year. Long after he was suspected as an evangelical, for example, Thomas Wyatt would continue to date his letters by church feasts. Daily life was also interwoven with the fabric of the church economically and ad-

ministratively, for while there were differences in official status between clerics and lay people, the administration of the church, like the administration
of the state, crossed back and forth, and so did money. Schools, universities,
and hospitals as well as the ubiquitous local chantries of fifteenth- and early
sixteenth-century England were clerical institutions founded and supported
by laymen's money. Money also passed the other way. Prebendaries and stew-
ardships were important sources of "church" income that could be received by
laymen—Wyatt held one. And the church owned at least one-fifth of the
land in England, putting many ecclesiastical establishments—most of the
church lands were concentrated in large holdings—on the same level as the
estates of the magnates. The livings of many parishes were also effectively in
the hands of the local lords and gentry, and the paths of preferment that
crossed the fabric of society inhabited by the Henrician court and church were
complex indeed; favors could be traded with both clerical and lay currency: in
1532, for example, one Mistress Bridget Hogan wrote to Cromwell to ask if
he could do anything in regard to the living of the parish of Uphall, which she
believed to be in the grant of Sir Henry Wyatt.[2]

There is no way of knowing whether Henry Wyatt's establishment of a
chantry was primarily a sincere act of piety or an appropriate social gesture for
it was undoubtedly both: the two are figures for one another, suspended together in social operation like Henry Wyatt's hands in the Holbein portrait, a
jewelled finger just touching the crucifix hanging from his heavy gold chain.
It is reductive to see such a necessary contradiction as mere hypocrisy. In matters of personal piety, then as now, it is difficult to separate the many motiva-
tions that are inscribed in acts of faith, whether conservative or radical. Even
the most general labels—such as protestant and catholic—are distinctly subject to warpage when applied to particular moments and individual historical
subjects in the 1520s and 1530s, for not only was theological discourse
drawn into complex intersection with the operation of family, generation, status, and politics, but there was the almost daily shifting of the range of belief
that was available as the rich and diffusive evangelism of the Continent
crossed to England in smuggled books and in the mouths of brilliant preachers like Tyndale and Barnes—only to be met with counterwaves of refutation
from agile and energetic conservatives like More and Fisher. And for the elite
and for those unlucky enough to be drawn into public controversy there was
the unstable royal politics of the court, where faction and religion and a royal
fancy for theology became impossibly entangled.

Thomas Wyatt appears to have negotiated these troubles without losing
his balance as a successful and loyal courtier of his king. He profited from the
distribution of monastic lands, the massive "nationalization" of property to

the king's use, but Cromwell's policy of policing the monasteries to "discover" corruption and make the transfer of property appear natural and inevitable had worked to make this sort of acquisition easy ideologically. The reports of the visitors to the monasteries were a discursive medium that allowed evangelical theology and the new doctrine of church and state to slide in on the coattails of the entrenched anticlericalism that traced the anxiety of power shared and divided between a worldly church and a pious world. Indeed, the priory of the Crutched Friars that Wyatt was granted in London came into the king's hands with a story that certified the greasy commerce between the cloister and the world and kept it ideologically safe by aligning it with a morally corrupt clergy. When six informers (city men antagonistic to the priesthood and eager to get what they could) found the prior in bed with a "whore" (most likely his long-time "concubine") at eleven o'clock in the morning of a Friday in Lent, he paid them thirty pounds to keep their information under wraps. When he later attempted to turn the tables by exposing their blackmail and "slander," the informers called his bluff by telling Cromwell.[3]

As I have suggested in my reading of "A spending hand," Wyatt knew the easy cadences of anticlerical satire, and his poem exposes some of the shallowness of estates rhetoric. But he is also clearly linked to the court faction that was discovering the uses of evangelical theology, a term often used of the early "protestantism" of France and perhaps useful here for its neutrality. The evangelical way of examining the relation of the believer to God also acted as a new counter in the distribution of power, both at court, where it animated the political faction of Anne Boleyn, and, to England's loss, in international politics. But it need not be an extreme position theologically, and it does not erase all of the traces of earlier inscriptions of theology in social practice such as devotion to Our Lady. Wyatt enjoyed playing extremes as an ambassador at the Catholic court of Charles, even to the point of drawing the attention of the Inquisition, but this posturing was accompanied by an acute sense of how much he could get away with and how circumspectly he must present himself. He was acutely aware of religious discourse as social. Mason and he had, for example, unsuccessfully implored Bonner and Heynes to show themselves at mass in Spain, "by cawse of the name that Inglysshe men then had to be all Lutherans . . . that we myght some tymes show our selves in the Churche togyther, that men conceavyd not an evell opynion of vs." Wyatt enjoys playing with a layering of irony here that evokes the unevenness and diffusiveness of religious expression. Bonner, then apparently a squeamish antipapist, refused to go to mass, even though as a priest he had a holy obligation to say mass daily. Now he has swung to the other side: "Yt was not lyke then that the Bysshope of Londone shulde sue to have the scripture in Inglyshe taken owt of the churche." And Bonner in a further irony is accusing Wyatt of being a papist in league with Cardinal Pole: "I thynke I shulde have much more adoe with a greate sorte in Inglonde to purge myselfe of suspecte of a Lutherane than of a Papyst."[4] Wyatt's stance here suggests an awareness that the practice of religion is not a simple matter of inward conscience but a form of public discourse; faith is not merely attending to an inward voice but speaking a language that voices many discourses.

A similar interest in the voicing of faith can be read in Wyatt's most important religious poems, his dramatic paraphrase of the seven penitential psalms, based in part upon Aretino's narrative paraphrase of 1534. In these paraphrases, Wyatt addresses the cultural gap that was exposed in the difficult years between the foundation of "Henry Wyatt's chantry" and the grant to Wyatt of the priory of the Crutched Friars. Wyatt's understanding of faith is mediated by a rhetoricity that figures the contradictions of faith not simply as a matter of theology but as a mode of behavior. The immediate interest of the psalms is a rhetoric that opens up some of the voices it speaks as the products of cultural disarray. In part, I believe, this is a result of Wyatt's self-conscious insertion of a line of political or moral criticism in the psalms; they address the scandal of Henry VIII, and, to some extent, they inscribe the ideological disruption of the times upon the king, figuring it as moral depravity. But in speaking the language of belief, the paraphrases reveal that the gap between discourses that is scandalous (criminal?) in the king is also a source of discomfort to his Christian subjects as they try to read their religious practice in the harsh new light of reform.

Like the three verse epistles, Wyatt's psalms are deeply engaged (and more than he could know) with the dense and contradictory cultural texts they transcribe. They are involved, of course, with the evangelical shifting of the religious paradigm, the re-formation of the church into a community of believers whose sinful nature is continually rewritten into faith through the reading of God's revelation in the Scriptures; a discourse where the sacrament is not a mystery of incorporation into the body of Christ but the commemoration or token of an event, the reinscription of the sign of the grace of God in Christ; a church that does not house images to serve as laymen's books but that joins in community laymen who read and interpret the books of Scripture themselves. And the psalms are also involved in the continuing reinscription of revelation in history, in the history of God's chosen Christian nations and of his faithful and faithless among them, for the play of Wyatt's rhetoric here implicates the difficult field of action that scriptural authority inscribes when its words are impersonated by the men and women who are

the church. The field of reference is personal, not theological or ecclesiologi-
cal. It is a matter of faith as subjection. The question that is posed by the rhetoric of Wyatt's penitential psalms and is not answered is "Who is speaking
the Scripture?" In the words of Wyatt's David in his translation of the pro-
logue to psalm 102:

> "Who hath expressed this thing?
> I, sinner, I! What have I said, alas?
> That God's goodness would within my song entreat
> Let me again consider and repeat."
>
> (152.13–16)

Who Speaks the Psalms?

There is a brief merry tale in Thomas More's *Dialogue concerning Heresies*
about an unchaste nun that "was gyven her in penaunce to say this verse:
Miserere mei deus, quoniam conculcauit me homo [Have mercy upon me,
God, for a man has trodden me underfoot] with a great threte that . . . [if]
she dyd so any more she sholde say the whole psalme."[5] The joke depends, of
course, precisely upon the question of who is saying the psalm. It brings into
question a conflict between the effectual faith of the individual believer and
the sacramental power of the penitential office. What good does it do simply
to "say" the words of a psalm in penance without experiencing inner repentance? This question, of course, embodies the fundamental conflict between
the late medieval sacramental view of penance and the emerging Lutheran
notion of the inward turning of the Christian away from sin toward salvation.
But the conflict antedates the Lutheran upheavals of the 1520s. It can be
read in the relation of lay Christians to the psalter in daily practice. The psalter is perhaps the scriptural text that was closest to lay devotion in the four-
teenth and fifteenth centuries. Psalters and prayer books containing the
psalms were common household items among the literate and propertied
classes, in richly illustrated manuscripts, simple working versions, and later in
printed texts. Anne Boleyn owned a beautifully illustrated French psalter,[6]
for example, and it would be surprising if Henry Wyatt did not commission
the best illuminated manuscripts he could afford to repose as memorials in
his chantry. The seven penitential psalms (6, 32, 38, 51, 102, 130, 143)
were a group of special importance in private devotion—they abound in devotional manuals and in translations into the European vernaculars. They
were used in daily devotion—sometimes, as John Fisher's sermons on the
penitential psalms and Alamanni's translation of the psalms suggest—in

connection with a meditation upon the seven capital sins. And they are closely connected with the preparation for death in times of adversity: Alamanni's preface explains (perhaps pro forma) that his translation springs from a close brush with dying suddenly and unprepared. They may have been employed liturgically as a preparation for the sacrament of penance, or, at times, set as an act of penance by the priest (the convention calls for them to be recited from an uncomfortable position). But they are most common as a private rhetoric of self-examination, an event not in liturgical life but in daily practice, invoked not by order of the church but as a response of the faithful Christian to the unfolding of God's providence in his life. They are private, if you will, in that they are recited or read alone. But, to be more precise, they are also a way of figuring the private life of faith in relation to the authoritative discourses, not only of the church, but of the other forms of public life. A miniature by Jean Maillard, to take a notorious example of the inwardness of the psalms being advertised, shows Henry VIII reading the psalms seated in his bed-chamber in the midst of a shaft of light from a lantern in the dome above, looking straight towards the viewer as he holds the book in his hands, while in the background the courtyard of his palace extends into the distance.

But if Henry's psalm book figures the supreme head, Wyatt's penitential psalms have all the marks of a form of composition that emerges as a therapeutic or even adversarial response, like the epigrams of stoic resistance and the neoclassical verse epistles. Scholars have hesitated between ascribing the psalms to the aftermath of Queen Anne's fall in 1536 and to the imprisonment of 1541. There would seem to be no guarantee for either date.[7] What scholarship can tell us, however, is that Wyatt's translation was engaged with the rich textuality of the penitential psalms as they were being continually rewritten in the early sixteenth century both in England and on the Continent, by evangelical scholars as well as by theological archconservatives. Wyatt was reading the latest things. He read a Latin paraphrase of the psalms from the Hebrew by a Hebrew scholar at Louvain, Johannes Campensis, published (1533) in a parallel text with a Latin translation by the Swiss reformer Uhlrich Zwingli as the *Enchiridion psalmorum* or *Handbook of the Psalms*. He consulted an English translation of Campensis (anonymous) and a translation of Zwingli by George Joye in *David's Psalter* (1534), as well as the version in the Coverdale Bible of 1535. He knew John Fisher's sermons on the psalms, which emphasized that the penitent sinner must overcome pride; and he also may well have known some of Tyndale's treatises. Alamanni's translations leave no traces in Wyatt's, although he certainly knew them from the *Opere Toscane* of 1532. But perhaps most important, he read a paraphrase of the psalms by Pietro Aretino, first published in 1534. Aretino provides a narrative frame for the psalms, setting them in the context of David's adultery, Uriah's death, and the prophesy of Nathan.

The story of David as the psalmist is ubiquitous, but Aretino rewrites the story of David and Bathsheba in his prose introduction to the psalms as a Petrarchan erotic epyllion. Cupid subverts David's kingly rule over himself and ultimately over his kingdom, blinding him with love when the "idol" of Bathsheba, the image of his beloved bathing, supplants the desire for the vision of God. The distorted, redoubling erotic phenomenology of metamorphosis that Aretino suggests in his mannered prose comes out fully in the terza rima stanzas of Wyatt's translation when Cupid enters David's vision and blinds him:

> Love, to give law unto his subject hearts,
> Stood in the eyes of Barsabe the bright,
> And in a look anon himself converts
> Cruelly pleasant before King David sight;
> First dazed his eyes, and further forth he starts
> With venomed breath, as softly as he might
> Touched his senses, and overruns his bones
> With creeping fire sparpled for the nonce.
>
> And when he saw that kindled was the flame,
> The moist poison in his heart he lanced
> So that his soul did tremble with the same.
> And in this branle as he stood and tranced,
> Yielding unto the figure and the frame
> That those fair eyes had in his presence glanced,
> The form that Love had printed in his breast
> He honour'th as thing of things the best.
>   (152.1–16)

I emphasize the images of conversion and the conversion of images here—of Cupid in Bathsheba's eye metamorphosizing or "converting" himself into a "look" that implants the image of Bathsheba in Solomon. I emphasize it because of the mirroring confusion it embodies, for it is not "really" Bathsheba in David's eye but Cupid "converted" into a look, and it is not clear who is looking. Does the "look" enter David's eyes because he is already a voyeur looking on? Or does Love's eroticized image of Bathsheba cause David to look? David and Bathsheba may be seeing one another reflected back and forth in their pupils—"looking babies" as the colloquial phrase goes—but only through the "imaginary" intervention of Cupid, who is supplanting the rule of King David with his own law, a perverse psychological rule that again makes fundamental assumptions about hierarchy and identity uncertain: who is the king and who the subject?

Questions of authority like this are part of the conventions of the penitential psalms. In the traditional medieval sacramental theology of penance, the penitent, having yielded to the false authority of his own lust and will, submits to the authority of God and is "converted" back to grace through a process of contrition, confession, and satisfaction in the sacrament of penance. The recital of the penitential psalms was supposed to be a dramatic rehearsal of the penitential process; and the story of David as the psalmist provides a type of the repentant sinner. But by inserting the psalms within the narrative frame, especially within a discursive context so alien as the Petrarchan imperium of Love, Aretino—and Wyatt with him—places David's words in the psalms within a social field, foreclosing the therapeutic identification of the penitent with the psalmist that the recital of the psalms demands as a devotional office.

The inwardness of Wyatt's paraphrases, then, is staged. David's entry into penitence is prompted by Nathan, the prophet who in effect "shames" the king into it, and part of the drama of David's psalmistry lies in the patent rhetoricity of his performance: David's slow process of "conversion" to grace is suspect. There are moments of credibility, of course, and perhaps of intensity, even in the first of the psalms in the sequence, when David has just thrown himself into penitence:

> Chastise me not for my deserving
> According to thy just conceived ire.
> O Lord, I dread, and that I did not dread
> I me repent, and evermore desire
> Thee, thee to dread. I open here and spread
> My fault to thee; but thou for thy goodness
> Measure it not in largeness nor in bread;
> Punish it not as asketh the greatness
> Of thy furor provoked by my offense.
> Temper, O Lord, the harm of my excess
> With mending will that I for recompense
> Prepare again; and rather pity me
> For I am weak and clean without defence.
>
> (81–93)

The suppleness of the line, the rise and fall of syntax and rhyme in Wyatt's terza rima, the alternation of "I" and "thee" here all suggest the yielding of the abject sinner to the immensity of God's grace. But, as Alexandra Halasz has recently established in a brilliant historiographical recontextualizing of Wyatt's psalms, the voice of David often proceeds "tactically rather than penitentially."[8] David asks for the Lord's mercy and then proceeds to argue that it is to the Lord's advantage to grant it, for what is mercy without someone to give it to, and if he is damned, he reasons, who will be left to tell the story of God's great mercy?

> Return, O Lord, O Lord I thee beseech,
> Unto thine old wonted benignity . . .
> . . . For if thy righteous hand that is so just
> Suffer no sin or strike with damnation,
> Thy infinite mercy want needs it must
> Subject matter for his operation.
> For that in death there is no memory
> Among the damned, nor yet no mention
> Of thy great name, ground of all glory,
> Then if I die and go whereas I fear
> To think thereon, how shall thy great mercy
> Sound in my mouth to the world's ear?
>   (116–36)

The figuring of the Word as voiced in David's mouth and heard in the "world's ear" betrays the calculation implicit in David's rhetoric. As Halasz eloquently states,

What is, in the psalmic original, a plea for mercy and an offer of praise . . . becomes, in the paraphrase, a negotiation involving two parties in the operation of justice. The basic plot, "making a deal with God," is present in the psalmic original, but the amplification, by developing at length why it is in God's interest to forgive David, emphasizes David's presumption. The suitor in this court speaks familiarly of the presiding judge . . . and presumes to offer him a deal. . . . The deal is made in chambers, as it were, away from the place where David is threatened, that is, as it were, away from the center of his princely power, his court.[9]

The drama of inwardness and repentance in Wyatt's paraphrase is one acted out in bad faith. The Petrarchan erotic conversions that contaminate the rhetoric of the opening narrative frame continue to contaminate the psalms themselves as David sings.

And Halasz tellingly points to a major difference between the narratives of Aretino and Wyatt. In the end of Aretino's narrative, just before the seventh penitential psalm, David has a vision of the Redemption, and becomes a type for Christ that foreshadows the Christian order in history. Wyatt continues his story beyond this moment of refiguration. In Wyatt's version, David reasons with the subtlety of one of Milton's fallen angels, asking the Lord for more. He supposes that the Lord, since he has already offered redemption to him, will also be happy to grant another small favor and will foreclose the rebellion of his son Absolon:

> "But of my sin since I my pardon have,
> My son's pursuit shall shortly be reject.
> Then will I crave with sured confidence."
> And thus begins the suit of his pretence.
> (723–26)

Not only does this arrogant David want to be saved, he wants to retain his kingdom intact, the rebellion that Nathan had foreseen having been given up ("reject") by Absolon. Wyatt's David, as Halasz argues, is unregenerate.

The last penitential psalm (143) follows this narrative link. It begins with lines in which David prays for the security of his kingdom, interpellated audaciously into the rhetorical fabric of the familiar incipit "Domini exaudi orationem meam":

> Hear my prayer, O Lord, hear my request.
> Complish my boon, answer to my desire
> Not by desert but for thine own behest
> In whose firm faith thou promised mine empire
> To stand stable.

The translation of "oratio" as "request," a legal term, is suspect enough, let alone the invocation of claims of "empire," a telltale word in a nation that had just recently laid claim to a Constantinian imperium in order to justify its new ecclesiology under the supreme headship of the king. But after this bold demand, the arrogance of the royal voice recedes into more contrite tones, and the sequence of psalms closes with the speaker rarely ironized unless by context, fearful of his own failure, respectful of the absolute power of God, grateful and secure in the knowledge that the Lord will confound his enemies.

This suspended closure, then, suggests the difficulty of understanding the larger rhetorical functions of the poem. It is easy enough to read the story of the unrepentant David—murdering his servant, seducing Bathsheba, conniving to hold on to his empire, all the while speaking Scripture like a choirboy—as an allegory of lust and violence and hypocrisy in Henry's household. David is a conventional figure for kings to assume or attain to— Henry's own psalter shows him at a table holding a harp, surrounded by the verses of the psalms, while to his side, slightly to the foreground of Henry, stands a household fool, his face a deformed parody of the king's. The miniature illustrates the verse "the fool saith in his heart that there is no God," and like Wyatt's paraphrase it is subject to the same inversion—who is the fool after all? Similar figurations of Henry as the willing tool of sycophants and the victim of his own lust and vanity can be found in many cultural productions from inside the court in the 1530s—Surrey's incisive character poem on Sardanapalus, for example, or the character of the profligate prince who suffers flatterers and dismisses his loyal servants in Thomas Elyot's dialogues, not to mention the great Turk invoked by the distanced figures who impersonate Thomas More in the *Dialogue of Comfort*. But the complexity of Wyatt's rhetoric, like that of Surrey and Elyot, lies in its failure to privilege the authority it inscribes. For despite the clear moralizing direction of the narrative frame and the occasional parodic disruptions in the penitential substance of the psalms, Wyatt's paraphrases still write a language of troubled inwardness. And Wyatt's hand is visible not only in the extensive revisions of the Egerton manuscript but in the dense and complex traces of his intervention in the textuality of the psalms, borrowing here from the Vulgate, here from Campensis or from Joye's psalter. Wyatt's interest in the psychology of conscience, or inward repining, is well known, and he too could figure his moral errors as "lust" not only in his letters to his son but in his inward-turning Petrarchan poems: "lust and trust's negligence." The paraphrase promises that the rhetoric of inwardness will be grounded in the authority of "Wyatt" the penitent, but it takes that promise back.

There may be, as Halasz argues, a self-conscious figuring of the position of the "author" in the paraphrases of the psalms. But the confusion of voices, in particular the impossible confusion of the oppressor with the victim, is ubiquitous in Wyatt's work. I have already remarked the work it performs in the verse epistles; here, despite the allegory of the Henrician court that is distinctly spelled out in the paraphrases of the psalms, the different voices of the psalms are perhaps not attributed entirely to authorial control but to the confusion of the subject. There are many voices that made "Thomas Wyatt" sound authentic. He "believed" in reform, in the gospel truth of the evangelicals; he "believed" in his country and could look forward to it being one day made whole in the faith of God, a new Zion. And it would be difficult to say that Thomas Wyatt did not "believe" in his king. More than circumspection holds Wyatt back from an unmitigated assault on the king; it is an ideological identification with the king's body that makes Wyatt too a part of David's impersonation of the penitent psalmist. David, or, for that matter, Henry is the failed type of the godly king of Zion—and as king, also a figure for his people. Wyatt too has failed to find an authentic space for his faith as it was rewritten in a new language. If the psalms condemn the lapses of Henry VIII, they also invite the reform of the kingdom. Even those faithful evangelicals committed to reform may not have heard their "own" voices speaking when they said the words of Scripture in a new language for the first time. When the script is being revised, it takes time to learn new lines, and the awkwardness of the actors becomes part of the history of the play; inscribed in the text as it is recited, the actors themselves are revising the script that they are struggling to come to terms with.

Scenes of Writing

Part of the appeal of Aretino's paraphrases to Wyatt was that they alienated the penitential psalms from what might have been an artificially pure theological context where there might be supposed an untroubled equivalence between words and faith. With a certain discursive violence, Wyatt's use of Aretino's frame inscribes the psalms from inside the alien discourse of Petrarchan erotic narrative and demonstrates that the language of faith too is embedded in an impure social process. It exposes faith as a language rather than as an unmediated form of truth. Part of the appeal of Petrarchan poetry itself to Wyatt lies in the inclusive variety, impurity, and divisiveness of its rhetoric.

The *Rime* are a heterogeneous rhetorical treasury of formal invention in figuration and prosody that license the appropriation of a wide range of material—popular, courtly, humanistic—to the production of an elite style that could set itself up against the classical wholeness and excellence it emulates and could open up a discursive authority for letters as a vehicle for personal rivalry and self-promotion in a courtly society.

In characterizing this kind of opportunistic appropriation of Petrarchism as a style, George Watson once remarked that to the Englishman of the sixteenth century, "Petrarch was a name rather than a book."[10] I think I should say, rather, that Petrarchan poetry prescribed a language, that it was a book from which one could learn a way of naming names. Learning how to speak this language was a form of empowerment: it represented the acquisition of the style we now identify with the renaissance. And learning how to "read" this book, moreover, provided a discursive means of recognizing and analyzing—albeit inadequately—the very kind of subjectivity it articulates.

Wyatt's appropriation of Petrarchan discourse is distinctly fragmentary and selective. The *Rime* are a sequence, and their exquisite patterns suggest how God reveals his order in man's fallen history. They articulate the subtle twists, thrusts, wandering, and grasping of a solipsistic psychology blocked by its own belated phenomenology from ever fully coming in contact with the "real." But Wyatt does not adapt the sequence as a model, and he rarely aspires to philosophical discursiveness. To him, as to all English poets before the mad flurry of sequences later in the century, the interest of Petrarch's model, whether the *Rime* themselves or the generations of its later imitations, was not sequential and synthetic but occasional. Rather than referring to one another as part of an intellectual system as do the poems in a sequence, the self-referentiality of Wyatt's erotic lyrics opens up a scene of writing that engages a play of reference with the social conditions of its articulation.

Wyatt's lyrics have often been called dramatic. The drama is one of rhetorical occasion. Again and again, the rhetoric of Wyatt's erotic poems invokes a specific event. He is drawn to Petrarchan models that specifically invoke a rhetorical moment. In "If amorous faith," for example, Wyatt translates very closely a sonnet that builds up a series of conditional clauses hypothesizing the speaker's suffering and finally breaks into an explosive rhetorical outburst:

> If a pale colour which love hath stained,
> If to have another than myself more dear,
> If wailing or sobbing continually,
> With sorrowful anger feeding busily,
> If burning afar off and freezing near
> Are cause that by love myself I destroy,
> Yours is the fault and mine the great annoy.
> (13.8–14)

The incremental rhetoric of the conceits here allows for an outburst at the close that in an imagined moment of reprisal reverts power to the speaker: the poem of suffering becomes one of blame. And the blame is staged as real. There is no doubt in Wyatt's lyrics that the rhetorical occasion is that of a man addressing a woman, not an idealized image of woman, but a woman who is there:

> Madam, withouten many words
> Once I am sure ye will or no;
> And if ye will, then leave your bourds,
> And use your wit and shew it so.

As Greene has remarked, "Within the poetic fiction, the speaker is truly responding to a second person who is responding to him, and the guarantee of this mutuality is the uncertainty."[11]

Blame is a frequent occasion of these lyrics. But the rhetorical mode can also be one of compliment. In a poem little remarked upon (because it remains so close to the social surface and thus does not seem to belong to the alienated "Wyatt" that has allowed his works to be read in the modern era), a speaker disdains the rich catalogue of gifts that might be fetched from afar as a New Year's gift for his lady because he has a gift close by:

> Nor I seek not to fetch it far;
> Worse is it not though it be nar.
> And as it is it doth appear,
> Uncounterfeit, mistrust to bar,
> Left whole and pure withouten peer,
> Dare I well say, the gift I give to year.
>
> To thee therefore the same retain.
> The like of it to have again
> France would I give it mine if were.
> Is none alive in whom doth reign
> Lesser disdain. Freely therefore, lo, here
> Dare I well give, I say, my heart to year.
> (101.12–24)

The language of social compliment here—Wyatt is working from the texts of Serafino, a poet of compliment par excellence—allows the speaker of this poem to contain doubt, counterfeit, and disdain in the elegance and grace of a moment of presentation, investing the occasion with the pathos of commitment.

The interest of this staging of the occasion in many of Wyatt's poems comes from the awareness they create of prior conditions. The speaker speaks the speech as it is told to him or he departs from it momentarily and to his cost. He behaves as he does even unwillingly because he does not know how else to make his choice. The very literariness of many of Wyatt's sonnets—their textual implication with their models—is often a means of marking the differing cultural conditions under which the two poems, model and imitation, were produced. Petrarch's *Rime,* of course, are also engaged with the historical conditions of their production. But the play of discourses that is articulated in the chronology and philosophical dilation of Petrarch's sequence tends to be focused in Wyatt's work, as in Marot's, for example, on the individual lyric positioned as a given historical moment of subjectivity, as a rhetorical place for the articulation of an egocentric awareness of the production of the subject.

And this slender rhetorical occasion is overloaded. The erotic exchange is inscribed by discourses that operate in contradiction inside of one another, confounding the spiritual, the aesthetic, and the political in the figuration of love and simulating in erotic breakdown a complex crisis in the space of the subject. Like stoic epigrams that are spoken as therapeutic responses to adversity, Wyatt's erotic poetry loads more upon the site of the personal—in this case love and its suffering—than the figure can sustain. The subject of Wyatt's erotic poems discovers himself, but he also discovers that he is speaking. The speaking subject can read "himself" as part of a script.

The first poem in the Egerton manuscript, for example, not only generates a specific occasion for the speaker's unhappiness that is not present in the Petrarchan text—his beloved's breaking of a "holy oath"—but analyzes the scene it stages:

> Behold, Love, thy power how she despiseth,
> My great pain how little she regardeth.
> The holy oath whereof she taketh no cure
> Broken she hath, and yet she bideth sure
> Right at her ease and little she dreadeth.
> Weaponed thou art and she unarmed sitteth.
> To thee disdainful her life she leadeth,
> To me spiteful without cause or measure.
>   Behold, Love.
>
> I am in hold. If pity thee moveth,
> Go bend thy bow that stony hearts breaketh
> And with some stroke revenge the displeasure
> Of thee and him that sorrow doth endure
>   And as his lord, thee lowly entreateth.
>   Behold, Love.

(1)

The speaker invites a perspective as if from the inside of the scene he projects: "Behold, Love." His use of the personified Love is analytical: it provides a way of staging his own erotic impulse as something that operates upon him. The speaker can analyze his subjection, but he cannot escape it. And in the closing line of this slight poem, just as the speaker is able to stage his own "displeasure" and "sorrow," distancing himself as "him," he also submits to the prior terms of his engagement: "and, as his lord, thee lowly entreateth."

Repeatedly, Wyatt's poems seem to reduce the meditative discursiveness and rich imagery of his Petrarchan models to a spare rhetoric of personal interaction much like the one projected in this poem. As Greene has argued, the figurative texture though which Petrarch's poems refer to one another and suggest the circular psychology of a philosophical consciousness is diminished and supplanted by a rhetoric that suggests a linear, unrepeatable event. The event is seen with baffled clarity by the speaker. The interest in this occasion lies in its incomplete and often inscrutable interrogation of its terms.

Wyatt's well-known imitation of *Rime* 140, "Amor che nel penser," translates the mythological scene of Love taking possession of the speaker's heart into an image of betrayal so fully realized in the military terms of knightly fealty that the military figuration that is a product of the speaker's wit in the original takes over the speaker and the poem:

> The long love that in my thought doth harbour
> And in mine heart doth keep his residence
> Into my heart presseth with bold pretence
> And therein campeth, spreading his banner.
> She that me learneth to love and suffer
> And will that my heart and lust's negligence
> Be reined by reason, shame and reverence,
> With his hardiness taketh displeasure.
> Wherewithal unto the heart's forest he fleeth,
> Leaving his enterprise with pain and cry,
> And there him hideth and not appeareth.
> What may I do when my master feareth,
> But in the field with him to live and die?
> For good is the life ending faithfully.
>
> (10)

The armed Cupid of Petrarch's poem is merely a figure for the aggressive sexuality of the speaker. It is a metaphor that the speaker controls. When his lady rejects his advances, he does not have the courage to press his cause. In the language of the metaphor, this rejection exposes Love as a braggart warrior. But the speaker has learned to live with the flickering of male desire, and he ends with a flippant dismissal of his own inadequacy both as a manly lover and as a moral agent: "Che poss'io tememdo il mio signore,/ se non star seco infin a l'ora estrema?/ che bel fin fa chi ben amando more" [What can I do when my Lord is afraid, except stay with him until the last hour? For he makes a good end who dies loving well]. Petrarch's military figure, then, is mock heroic. But Wyatt's version takes the military metaphor seriously. His poem tells the story of a single recent event in the erotic experience of the speaker. The military metaphors provide a medium for analyzing the agonizing moral choice of the speaker not to renounce his "lust's negligence" even though he recognizes it as cowardly and as wrong—at the cost of being lost in the "heart's forest." He does so because he does not know any other way to behave, because he cannot step outside of his metaphor. The occasion of the poem, then, the rhetorical drama of its staging, focuses the poem on the very language with which the speaker comes to understand his situation, the deeply embedded terms of service and personal loyalty.

The rhetorical occasions of Wyatt's erotic lyrics make them recede into their inaccessible origins; they place the poems in the foreground as scenes of writing, and they produce the tantalizing trace of the hand that inscribes them. They are autobiographies without a referent. In one Petrarchan imitation, for instance, the historical exempla of Caesar's false tears for Pompey and of Hannibal's laughter in defeat contaminate the projection of the speaker's feigned "sport and play":

> Caesar, when that the traitor of Egypt
> With th'honourable head did him present,
> Covering his gladness, did represent
> Plaint with his tears outward, as it is writ.
> And Hannibal eke, when fortune him shut
> Clean from his reign and from all his intent,
> Laughed to his folk whom sorrow did torment,
> His cruel despite for to disgorge and quit.
> So chanceth it oft that every passion
> The mind hideth by colour contrary
> With feigned visage, now sad, now merry;
> Whereby if I laughed any time or season,
> It is for because I have no other way
> To cloak my care but under sport and play.
>   (9)

All that the speaker leaves unsaid, the reasons for his deception of others or for his mind's deception of him, defers to the exempla. The inwardness of the sestet is suspended, incompletely and unsatisfactorily predicated upon the story of public deception. And what relation do they bear to one another? Does Caesar illustrate the speaker's feigning? Or does the example of royal deception trickle down from the top, making it a necessary survival skill for Caesar's servants? Is this a poem of loss in love? Vellutello's commentary suggests that Petrarch was mourning Laura. Or is there some other loss? A personal defeat? A lost friend? The death of a disgraced patron? Both? Fillefo's commentary suggested that Petrarch's occasion was his brother's death, when he hid his grief.[12] All?

One of Leland's memorial verses in *Naeniae* describes an image on Wyatt's signet ring that circles around the problem of example and subject here. The ring figures the complex engagement of the speaker's subjectivity and the public social authorities that circulate in its production. For the sign on Wyatt's ring was Caesar's head:

> Annulus in digito solitus radiare Viati
> Fabre factus erat gemmaque superbus achate
> Caesaris effigies in qua verissima Juli,
> Sculpta, occludendis signum spectabile chartis
> Caesaris ad summam virutem calcar imago
> Ingenitas auxit vires animosque Viati.

[The ring that always glittered on Wyatt's finger was skillfully made and boasted an agate stone on which was carved the truest likeness of Julius Caesar, a notable token for sealing up his letters. The image of Caesar, a spur to the greatest virtue, magnified Wyatt's inborn strength and spirit.]

To be able to wear Caesar, to possess him in miniature, to carry him on his finger, to seal letters, marking them as his own with the head of Caesar suggests a more complex relation than Leland's didactic explanation supplies. The identification of the servant with the master represents both an internalizing of the ideology of power and the will to interrogate it.

This complex identification is one of the layers of inscription that riddles the poem that has become one of the foundations of the current Wyatt canon, "Whoso list to hunt." In this poem it is not the speaker who is "signed" by Caesar in jewelry but his lost beloved:

Whoso list to hunt, I know where is an hind,
But as for me, helas, I may no more.
The vain travail hath wearied me so sore,
I am of them that farthest come behind.
Yet may I by no means my wearied mind
Draw from the deer, but as she fleeth afore
Fainting I follow. I leave off therefore
Sithens in a net I seek to hold the wind.
Who list her hunt, I put him out of doubt,
As well as I may spend his time in vain.
And graven with diamonds in letters plain
There is written her fair neck round about:
"Noli me tangere for Caesar's I am,
And wild for to hold though I seem tame."

The wild irony of the closing couplet focuses on the problem of what it means to be "Caesar's." In Petrarch's fragile vision (*Rime*, 140), the speaker recollects a moment on the verge of spiritual fulfillment, standing still in the cold of fall as a white doe appeared in the green grass, only to disappear into the waters of the stream. Reading the inscription on her collar just before the deer vanishes, the speaker sees: "Nessun mi tocchi, al bel collo d'intorno/ scritto avea di diamanti et di topazi./ Libera farmi al mio Cesare parve" ["Let no one touch me," she bore written with diamonds and topazes around her lovely neck. "It has pleased my Caesar to make me free"] (9–11). Petrarch is drawing upon a traditional story of Caesar's white stags being found living three hundred years after his death with collars bearing the inscription, "Noli me tangere, Caesaris sum." The immortal deer thus belongs to God, jumping out of the speaker's sight as the bright light of midday yields to the setting sun.

In Wyatt's translation, the hunt figures sexual pursuit. His speaker addresses an audience of men, of fellow hunters. And the poem is poised at a moment when the speaker is just on the verge of giving up his frustrating pursuit of a woman who has eluded him. The deer (dear) does not idealize the woman, but figures her teasing sexuality, her intermittent signals of availability and denial. And Caesar is not God, but the powerful monarch who has claimed possession of the lady and inscribed her body with his name. Caesar has not brought the deer the freedom of eternal life, but has bought her a necklace of diamonds that marks her not as steadfast and enduring like Petrarch's diamond and topazes, but as "his."

And yet Wyatt translates Petrarch's "Nessun mi tocchi" not into English but back into Latin, recalling the biblical words of the unrisen Jesus as he appeared to Mary Magdalene at the sepulchre: "Do not touch me, for I am not yet ascended to the Father." Even as the speaker is cynically reading the inscription as the mark of Caesar's sexual property, he (or is this the "author"?) is setting in motion that contradictory Christian frame of reference. The deer is "Caesar's," but who is Caesar? As so many readers have noticed, Wyatt's entire poem is suspended between contradictory frames of reference. Its words are notoriously unstable. If the adjective "wild," for example, is predicated upon a woman, it may suggest her unmastered erotic energy—an energy "untamed" by her possession by Caesar (who is thus emasculated). If applied to a deer, the adjective "wild" suggests shying away (and hence chastity).

The unstable words of the poem thus circulate around a scene of writing that opens up the speaker's rhetoric. He has focused his rhetoric on the contested possession of the lady. But the rhetorical interest of his words also falls upon how the speaker is mastered. The rhetorical occasion of the poem in a way makes the hunting metaphor of Petrarch's poem literal, for the speaker addresses the male fellowship of the hunt, the mob of gentlemen who pursue both deer and women, and who like to talk about the triumphs and (always understandable) failures of the pursuit in the jocund laughter of shared self-congratulation. The speaker engages the many competing discourses that are inscribed in production of the court. In some ways, the rhetoric of the poem investigates the speaker's relation to Caesar, for it is he (the speaker) who would appear to be "Caesar's" even more than the spirited woman who wears his necklace. The poem begins with cocky confidence, "I know where is an hind." But it does not ever fully reveal the answer because the words cannot be said out loud. The speaker claims to have understood his experience and to have put it behind him ("I put him out of doubt"), but he is still among the pack of hunters as he speaks in frustration: "I am of them that farthest come behind." Rhetorically he is a part of the language that he speaks. He can name Caesar, but he is also a subject of Caesar and a creature of God, "named" by these different authorities. His voice is overloaded. No act of will can produce a unified subject from it. We should remember perhaps that one of the reasons this poem works so well is that it can be read as a joke. It does not have to take itself seriously. Imagine it spoken by a speaker who uses his own impotence (political and sexual) to magnify the king's acquisition of his latest prize, who enjoys a moment of ribald laughter as he reminds a group of men that "some goods can't be touched, and oh, there's a loss, for she's a piece of work."

Anne Boleyn has often been supposed to have been the lady of this poem, an historical allegory that makes considerable sense, but that does not perhaps enhance the reading of the poem, for the rhetoric of the poem is not secured any more by historical reference than it is by biblical allusion. Anne can, however, provide a convenient example of how the discursive confusion projected in "Whoso list" could be inscribed upon the subjects of the Henrician court. In the days after Anne's arrest, for example, John Husee, the tenacious and sharp agent for the Lisle family at court, wrote home to Lady Lisle with the news that Anne was being called every name in the book of bad women: "Madam, I think verily, if all the books and chronicles were totally revolved, and to the uttermost persecuted [prosecuted] and tried, which against women hath been penned, contrived, and written since Adam and Eve, those same were, I think, verily nothing in comparison of that which hath been done and committed by Anne the Queen." To Husee the ideology of traditional antifeminism is transparent here, and he ironically comments with his legal metaphor on the ideological susceptibility of the law. But he still believes that she is guilty: "which though I presume be not all thing as it is now rumored, yet that which hath been by her confessed, and others, offenders with her, by her own alluring, procurement and instigation, is so abominable and detestable that I am ashamed that any good woman should give ear thereunto. I pray God give her grace to repent while she now liveth. I think not the contrary but she and all they shall suffer."[13] The ideology of state justice with its exemplary procedures of voluntary confession, the credibility of a lady and a queen, the horror of sexual crime—Husee is surely speaking of Anne's alleged incest with her brother—prevent Husee from reading the scene any other way. He was also certain that Wyatt was going to die.

Anne Boleyn continued to be inscribed in history as English men and women looked back on her story as one of either a whore or a martyr, her biography made to bear the freight of all the great matters of state, religion, and biological accident that contributed to her fall (there is surely no causality either ideological or willful in miscarriage or infertility). But overloading the site of the subject was the social process that made brilliant figures like Anne work in Tudor culture; and it is perhaps not surprising that she is written in history as the woman who brought the latest styles from France and the evangelical zeal for reform to court with her in her suitcase. In the personal politics of the court, of course, her charm and her sexuality counted. And these were matters that were both generated and (unsuccessfully in the end) controlled by ideological production.

Consider the pageants prepared from texts written by Leland and Nicholas Udall for the entry of the proud pregnant bride into London after her marriage. In a hastily constructed "castle" topped by a cupola was a chamber whose ceiling was painted to represent the heavenly bodies. From a green field on the ground rose a swelling mound on the top of which stood the stock of a tree, a fertile ground impregnated to produce a noble race. The pageant, on the other hand, figured the pregnancy in Christian terms. To one side of the hill sat Saint Anne, the mother of the mother of God, the fertile and nurturing woman whose womb connected Jesus to the root of Jesse. Saint Anne was surrounded by her progeny. The two mothers, the Virgin Mary and Mary Cleophas, mother of Saint James and Joses, sit to one side. Her third daughter, Mary Salome, with her husband and four children sit to the other side. One of the children carries a placard inscribed with a message from the City: "We the Citizens by you in short space / Hope such issue and descent to purchase."[14]

As Husee's letter proves, the danger of the inscription of so many discourses onto the site of the subject is that they can so easily be shifted. But at the level of the subject, this ideological production can be seamless. I mentioned in chapter 1 that Anne Boleyn had signed her book of hours with a poem for Henry VIII. Let us look now at the text and context of that inscription. It appears in her book of hours beneath a richly illuminated picture of the Virgin Mary, with Gabriel at her side, attending to the news of the Incarnation. Anne, hoping for pregnancy, wrote some dutiful wifely verses: "Be daly prove you shalle me fynde, / to be to you bothe lovynge and kynde."[15] How better for a woman of power to hope for a royal child? How better to invite her sanctimonious royal husband to bed?

There is not necessarily a shadow of falseness in Anne's verses. The ideology of productions like Anne's entry pageant works because she and other people believed it. And to attribute Anne's verses to calculation or hypocrisy assumes that people always know what they are doing. But poems like "Whoso list to hunt" capitalize on the potential slippage between the public mobilization of heavily ideologized discourses and the private will to introspection. They address not so much the falseness of the ideology, or the willful deceptiveness of the individual subject, but the inauthenticity of the "person" named by that ideology. In considering one final poem, another set piece of the Wyatt canon, "They flee from me that sometime did me seek," I should like to consider the potential for inauthenticity that is part of the structure of private life. The poem is a virtual stage set for the operation of the personal politics of the royal household. Its setting in the private chambers behind the great hall shows the "personal" being produced in opposition to others:

> They flee from me that sometime did me seek
> With naked foot stalking in my chamber.
> I have seen them gentle, tame, and meek
> That now are wild and do not remember
> That sometime they put themself in danger
> To take bread at my hand; and now they range
> Busily seeking with a continual change.
>
> (80.1–7)

The chamber here is produced as a place of personal authenticity: it is "my" place; it belongs to the speaker. But that private place, and the "person" that it belongs to, are set up only in opposition to the same scene perceived as social. We know about the "I" only what he says about others, and his words collapse against one another, echoing hollowly in the chamber. The difference between then and now is not a matter of values—nothing has changed about "them" except the relation of "them" to the speaker. "Gentle, tame, and meek" mean nothing more than that "they" were on "my side"; "wild" that they are not. The speaker's animal metaphors remove the frame that moral discourse might impose: there are no good or bad animals, just those that bite and those that do not bite. The "naked foot" that might promise a shared secrecy or even an intimacy reveals nothing. And the chamber from which the speaker addresses the reader, exposing himself, is also a brittle disappointment. There is nothing there.

"They" in this first stanza "do not remember" their former intimacy with the speaker, and the poem from the start is about memory and about forgetting. The speaker too is remembering, and his memory is perhaps just as blank and amoral as "theirs." In the second stanza he presents a memory that he is thankful for:

> Thanked be fortune it hath been otherwise
> Twenty times better, but once in special,
> In thin array after a pleasant guise,
> When her loose gown from her shoulders did fall
> And she me caught in her arms long and small,
> Therewithal sweetly did me kiss
> And softly said, "Dear heart, how like you this"?
>
> (8–14)

The opening lines of this stanza invoke the shared world of courtly ideals. They are the words of Chaucer's Troilus and they suggest the resilience in fortune that "gentle" men and women must sustain, insisting upon their "identity" against the anonymous forces they oppose in "Fortune." But the speaker's treasured memory is also an act of suppression, for as he dwells with loving detail upon the remembered substance of that brief nocturnal assignation, he does not hear the implications of his own words or see the thinness of the scene. This whole scene collapses into words that are blank social placeholders, the polite fillers of courtly exchange. The speaker describes the "thin array" of his visitor as "after a pleasant guise." He remarks that her arms were "long and small," and while he says that they "caught" him his memory suppresses the entrapment implied by his language and savors only the pleasure of the embrace.

The much remarked passivity of the speaker, then, allows the poem to close without recoiling from this memory. The lovers part with words that do not address their situation: "And I have leave to go of her goodness, / And she also to use newfangleness" (18–19). In another context, a word like "newfangleness" might mobilize a moral critique. But here—suggesting something like "whatever damn thing she pleases"—it is merely another index of the speaker's lassitude. "It was no dream," he claims, "I lay broad waking" (18). But in a sense this speaker does not know the difference between waking and dreaming. His waking life is lived as an unconscious experience, as a signifier that he does not control and that he cannot understand.

But the poem does not really "end" with the speaker. The sharply defined progression of its three stanzas, the play of allusions to the shared texts of courtly culture, to the dream visions and elevated language of romance, the intimate realism of the setting in the chamber—all these mark the poem as the cultural work of an insider who is also an author: the sophistication of the poem promises an understanding that goes beyond the passivity of the speaker. The poem produces an "author." And it also produces (or suppresses) a scene of writing. For as C. E. Nelson pointed out in a thoughtful note published in 1963,[16] "They flee from me" evokes not only the polite social exchanges of courtly love in the *Troilus,* but the erotic discourse of Roman elegy. This is a bedroom poem. The courtly "realism" of its setting in the chamber is in fact written from Ovid's *Amores,* and from a poem so scandalous that when the Loeb edition was published in 1914 the editors did not translate it and placed it out of order at the end of the volume.

Amores 3.7, as Nelson remarks, is an "impotency farce." The girl may not have been beautiful, the speaker admits in the opening of the poem, she may not have been well-bred, she may not even have been one that he had longed for. But she was there in his bed:

hanc tamen in nullos tenui male languidus usus,
  sed iacui pigro crimen onusque toro;
nec potui cupiens, pariter cupiente puella,
  inguinis effeti parte iuvante frui.
illa quidem nostro subiecit eburnea collo
  bracchia Sithonia candidiora nive,
osculaque inseruit cupide luctantia femur,
  et blanditias dixit dominumque vocavit,
et quae praeterea publica verba iuvant.

[Nonetheless it was her I was holding and I was limp and good for nothing. I lay on the motionless bed, a reproach and a useless burden to it. I could not do it, even though I wanted her and she likewise wanted me, without the help of my worn-out prick. She threw her arms around my neck, whiter than Thracian snow, and drove down deep eager kisses as our tongues wrestled one another, and she put her playful thigh between mine. She spoke sweet nothings in my ear and called me master and all the other usual words that help.] (my translation)

When nothing seems to work, the insulted girl wraps her loose gown about her and hurries out on her naked feet: "nec mora, desiluit tunica velata soluta—/ et decuit proripuisse pedes." Nelson goes on to show other similarities, such as *Amores* 1.5, in which the speaker recalls being in bed in the middle of a summer day, when Corinna enters dressed in her loose gown ("tunica velata recincta").

Wyatt's poem "remembers" the erotic arousal, the pornographic details of the white arms, the loose gown, the kiss, the enticing speech. But it "forgets" the impotence of the man. The memory is cut off, as it often is in other Ovidian elegies, just before the moment of climax. But was there a climax in the remembered scene? Or does the poem suppress the impotence figured in its source? Is the speaker's "passivity" a figure for the suppressed physical impotence of Ovid's poem? Does Wyatt's speaker have to persuade himself that his memory was real? Is self-persuasion the function of the lingering language of the memory of the bedroom scene in the central stanza? Is this a moment of pornographic replay? Is this scene of sexual arousal a dream after all? Does the speaker *now* lie "broad waking" in bed after an erotic fantasy?

I do not know. This poem has all the engagement with its source that Greene finds in "Stand whoso list," but it can hardly be called a "heuristic" imitation. The "author" recedes from his poem as mysteriously as does his speaker. The intense intimacy of the poem never delivers the "person" it names. The scene of writing staged by the quality of the poem as a made object never produces the "person" who made it. The "author" too is a cultural function, and the "scene" of writing is staged. The hand of Thomas Wyatt is visible here, but it is not always legible. For the historical "Thomas Wyatt" is also part of a script he did not write. He could not always understand the languages he was learning to transcribe and he does not know the revisions he has made in the script.

Postscript

Since his death, the hand of Thomas Wyatt has been rediscovered in many different readings. For Surrey, as for Leland and for Wyatt's other contemporary elegists, I have suggested, his hand was a convenient figure for the new "renaissance" cultural constellation of the author of national letters, a man of natural excellence who speaks for his nation and against his nation's vices. These elegies were published, but they still emanate from the inner circle of court as courtiers tried out their ambitions upon a larger national field, testing the new medium of print in "limited editions." When Richard Tottel published Wyatt's and Surrey's works in *Songs and Sonnets* (1557), he inaugurated another cultural circuit in the reading of these poems.

Tottel was a rich London printer whose business expanded rapidly when he secured the royal monopoly on printing law books, a highly saleable product in this litigious culture.[1] Tottel's other publishing ventures show him appealing to the same clientele: the educated and fashionable aspirants to success drawn to London (to the Inns of Court, among other institutions) in increasing numbers as the city and its court became the center for the distribution of power. From Tottel's presses came editions of such staples of aspiring provincial taste as Lydgates's *Fall of Princes* and Hawes's *Pastime of Pleasure,* and, in the same year as *Songs and Sonnets,* the massive folio edition of another new London author, the English works of Thomas More. Between 5 June and 31 July 1557 Tottel sold out three editions of *Songs and Sonnets.* By 1587, six more editions had been published. Tottel promises his status-hungry readers treasures previously hoarded by gentlemen in manuscript, and in doing so his edition produces a Thomas Wyatt curiously removed from the historical context of the Henrician court. The Thomas Wyatt that Tottel was providing was a formal example. Topical references dangerous in Marian England were expunged. And, more important, the poems were regularized according to the editor's or editors' metrical preferences (changing frequently in the linguistic instability of this mobile culture), and they were ordered in a seminarrative literary sequence, headed by titles like "The lover hopeth of better chance" ("He is not dead") or "Of others' feigned sorrow and the lover's feigned mirth" ("Caesar when that the traitor").

After the publication of *Songs and Sonnets,* Wyatt's and Surrey's poems were imitated often and variously among a much larger readership.[2] They circulated among aspiring courtiers—both men and women—and, as broadside ballads, among the working people on the London street. They were parodied and bowdlerized as moralistic verse, a sure sign of a wide circulation. But Wyatt and Surrey were among the "authors" of English poetry even as the circumstances under which Wyatt and Surrey had produced their poems at the Henrician court receded into obscurity and the names "Wyatt" and "Surrey" became synecdoches for a body of work. "I repute them," states Puttenham's *Art of English Poesy,* "for the two 'chiefe lanternes of light to all others that haue since employed their pennes vpon English Poesie.'"[3] And between them, the *Art* continues, "I finde very little difference."

The works of Wyatt and Surrey entered into polite obscurity in the seventeenth century. Other authors replaced them as inaugural "lanterns" (Spenser, Sidney, Shakespeare, Jonson), for by the time of Milton the canon of English letters had grown by several prolific generations. By the middle of the eighteenth century, the poetry of Wyatt had become an English antiquity, the object of curiosity for scholarly gentlemen. In 1760, for example, the poet Thomas Grey transcribed Wyatt's defense of 1541 for publication among Horace Walpole's *Miscellaneous Antiquities.* When Walpole finally published the oration in 1772, he did not fail to advertise its illustrious transcriber, his labor an "homage of justice paid to a genius, his predecessor."[4] Walpole himself provided a biography of Wyatt, but the venture was not notably successful, and Walpole sold less than a fifth of his run, commenting that "if Sir Thomas had abused Cranmer and Latimer instead of Bonner, he would have been more fashionable."[5] Bishop Percy had planned an edition of Wyatt and Surrey under the prompting of the printer Jacob Tonson in 1763 and had worked on it sporadically until the sheets were finally destroyed in a fire in 1808. Tonson was probably hoping to capitalize upon a brief flurry of interest in Surrey. Pope had praised him in "Windsor Forest" as the "Granville of another age." Indeed, Surrey's reputation rose above Wyatt's in this neoclassical era. Thomas Warton praises him as the "first English classical poet," and throughout the nineteenth century Surrey was ranked as the more accomplished of the two Henrician poets, because his verses were perceived to be more polished and his style more polite.[6]

The great edition of Wyatt and Surrey completed by the Reverend George Frederick Nott in 1815 and 1816 was, like Bishop Percy's abortive venture, the product of a gentleman's leisure and erudition. Nott was an ambitious cleric—a tutor of Princess Charlotte who was dismissed for trying to wheedle a bishop's miter out of his position at court. He won some notoriety by attacking Byron's *Cain* as heretical in a sermon—thus winning himself verses beginning "Do you know Dr. Nott"—and he was justifiably embarrassed when he was thought to have impugned Shelley's reputation when preaching in Pisa in 1821. This imputation was much to Mary Shelley's regret (she had had some share in spreading the rumor), and she made every effort to dispell interest in the charge by dutifully attending Nott's services at least once a month. But Nott seems to have had a gift for inviting controversy. As Mary Shelley reports, he preached against atheism after especially inviting her to attend, and "this appeared to me very important and I wrote to him to ask him whether he intended any personal allusion, but he denied the charge most entirely—this affair among the English at Pisa made a great noise, the gossip here is of course out of all bounds."[7]

I cite the incident to suggest how far removed from the literary scene of the Shelleys and their circle Wyatt's poetry had become in the early nineteenth century, for it was an antiquarian rather than a "poetic" interest that brought men like Nott to study Wyatt's work and apply to these crabbed manuscripts and tattered volumes the vast erudition of their hours in the study. And, indeed, Nott's identification of Wyatt's sources—classical, continental, and Chaucerian— is almost unsurpassed. Nott did not labor entirely alone. Wyatt's political problems of 1541 again became a matter of some historical interest when Bonner's accusation was discovered by John Bruce, along with some other Wyatt documents, and published in the *Gentleman's Magazine* in 1850.[8] Wyatt's works also circulated in many of the standard library editions of English poets. Tennyson's friend Francis Palgrave included lyrics by Wyatt and Surrey in the *Golden Treasury*, a book frequently found in the Victorian household.

The Victorian scholarship on Wyatt was increasingly professionalized, and as these scholars (following the Darwinian model of Shakespeare's life) looked anew at the documents, Wyatt was given an artistic "career." The professional production of Wyatt began with some extensive German scholarship in the 1880s and 1890s and came into full flower with the publication of Agnes Foxwell's *Study of Sir Thomas Wyatt's Poems* (1911) and her edition, the *Poems of Sir Thomas Wiat* (1913), the first edition since Nott to contend with the problem of the Wyatt manuscripts at length. The bias of this early scholarship is distinctly aesthetic and progressive. William Simonds, for example, classifies Wyatt's poetic development into six different stages, leading to a late period of deeper religious and philosophical insight. In 1903, a German scholar named Egon Wintermantel adapted Simonds's categories to a progressive reading of Wyatt's poems as a sequence of literary compliments directed toward Anne Boleyn. Foxwell viewed the versions of Wyatt's poems in the Devonshire, Arundel and Egerton manuscripts as artistically progressive, leading toward stylistic perfection particularly in metrical matters, and to a greater maturity and elegance in expression.[9]

E. M. W. Tillyard's modern spelling edition of Wyatt in 1929 produced Wyatt as a poet worth reading for a wider audience of English students. And when Wyatt is restored as an English author for the wider middle-class literacy of the twentieth century, an atavistic bias in twentieth-century scholarship turns quickly toward what it identified in Wyatt's work as "native." In 1897 William Courthope had found Wyatt best when working unhampered by foreign sources, and for Tillyard, Wyatt's native lyrics look back to the spontaneity of medieval song and forward to the roughness of Donne. By midcentury, readings of Wyatt's poetry had fallen into the lines of a literary cold war, whether one takes Ivor Winters' modernist invocation of a "plain" style as opposed to a "golden" style or C. S. Lewis's apocalyptic vision of a "golden" Elizabethan age emerging from the shadows of a "drab" age.[10]

This interest in the native runs parallel to a twentieth-century interest in the "genuineness" of Wyatt, an interest in the honesty his poems embody, in the inwardness that they express. In much New Critical work of the 1950s and 1960s, this inwardness is distinctly associated with a persona, with the rhetorical production of a voice, and in the most influential of this work— thoughtful essays, for example, by Arnold Stein and Donald Friedman— one begins to see the characteristic rhetorical complexity of the twentieth-century Wyatt. And it is a complexity that reflects the moral ambiguities of middle-class life in the West after World War II. At times, these critical works make Wyatt speak as the voice of the alienated intellectual, attributing to him an existential unwillingness to accept any terms except those of personal struggle against the intractable world outside. Even Wyatt's supposedly irregular metrical practice—long the bane of his apologists—can be read as a sign of integrity.

At the same time, however, the scholarly community was also becoming increasingly aware of the circumstances of Wyatt's poetic composition. Ruth Hughey, Hyder Rollins, and Raymond Southall produced a great deal of information about how Wyatt's manuscripts circulated; H. A. Mason uncovered new material on Wyatt's use of humanist sources; Patricia Thomson explored the Petrarchan influence; Sergio Baldi demonstrated the neoclassicizing bent of Wyatt's Italian sources; and John Buxton provided a reminder of the courtly context. Muir's "Life and Letters" volume made Wyatt's personal and official correspondence available, and the edition of Wyatt's poems by Muir and Thomson, for all its faults (mainly transcription errors and inflation of the canon through dubious attribution), made a contextualizing commentary available. Despite disagreements over particulars, the editions of Richard Harrier, Joost Daalder, and Ronald Rebholz provide general directions for treating the problem of the canon.

The most recent work on Wyatt deploys an increasingly rhetoricized historiography and a historicized reading of literature, maintaining an awareness of unstable rhetorical structures used by men and women in the past and by contemporary historians (wittingly and unwittingly) as they construct the past. What had been viewed in part as problems of literary voice or moral problems of personal selfhood or identity, as aesthetic problems of the genuine and the artificial convention, are now seen as part of the larger problems of the ideological production of the subject, and Wyatt is one of the canonical figures in the postmodern inscription of the sixteenth century as a period of crisis or change in the process of subjection, a crisis of which the rise of literature is as much a symptom as a cause. To Stephen Greenblatt, Wyatt plays with the competing forms of domination and submission—to the king, to the church, to the word of God—dramatizing a suspension between "self-fashioning" and the world that fashions the self. Wyatt stands in Greenblatt's historical allegory of sixteenth-century English culture between the self-fashioning of Thomas More, who inscribed himself and his opposition to the king through submission to the supreme consensus of the church, and William Tyndale, who surrendered to the Word of God as he translated and promulgated it.

Earlier allegories, of course, are always quaintly dated. In 1922, for example, Eleanor Hammond argued that Wyatt sometimes "signed" poems by inscribing anagrams (IWATT, AIWT, etc.) in the initial letters of stanzas.[11] And in 1961, Ethel Seaton—who had spent fifty years as a well respected member of the academic establishment—published *Sir Richard Roos, c. 1410–1482, Lancastrian Poet*, in which she argues that single and double acrostic anagrams as well as verbal parallels establish that most of the poems now ascribed to Wyatt, as well as about half of those ascribed to Surrey, were written by Roos in the mid-fifteenth century.[12] To me the recent sifting and resifting of the "evidence" in an effort to prove or disprove the consummation of sexual relations between Wyatt and Anne Boleyn is equally quaint, and like the Catholic accounts to prove consummation or the Protestant ones to disprove it, extraordinarily revealing of cultural preoccupations (sexual as well as theological). But I should not want to foreclose any avenue of inquiry prematurely. Sixteenth-century accounts of Lady Anne and Sir Thomas are rich sources for the study of the complex ideological inscriptions of sexuality, for example. Indeed, my own caution in adding my efforts to the study of Thomas Wyatt's life and letters would be not that we delight in discrediting outmoded allegories but that we respect the many avenues of historical agency and the necessary incompleteness of writing history. I exercise this caution not because I am yearning for a complete, whole past that is somehow "back there" and that is irrecoverable, but in order to encourage a present practice of historiography that is alert to change and complexity in the embeddedness of social process and that encourages the reading of difference in the written fabric of history.

Let me close with an inscrutable story. In 1555 a Spanish physician named Don Andrés de Laguna who had just retired as papal physician to Julius II published an annotated translation of Dioscorides's *Materia medica*. In chapter 3, which concerns the physiology of cocks and hens, Laguna recalls in his notes a visit to the cockpit at Whitehall while on a visit to England in 1539. The amphitheater was surrounded by cages belonging to important men of rank. In the center of the pit stood a stout wooden column upon which the cocks were placed. The jewels and coin bet on them were placed in between the contestants. The cocks, according to Don Andrés, fight with the valor of honorable warriors, and their virtues are respected by their owners— specially salaried physicians are summoned to attend to the wounded and dying. But Don Andrés is nonetheless appalled by the waste of effort:

As I was spending my time in this manner in the company of certain English gentlemen, I told them that it seemed to me great childishness and rather vulgar to esteem such a thing so highly. A knight called Thomas Huuyat came up, a man of rare wit who had been ambassador for some years at the Imperial court. He answered me as a spokesman for all of them. "There is nothing more serious, more useful, or more worthy of praise in any well constituted republic," he said. "Leaving aside the diversion which the contest affords, I say that there is not a single prince or a captain one might find among the spectators who, contemplating how fervently these little animals seek for victory at the expense of their own lives and with no profit in view, even if he were of a cowardly nature, would not recover a positive strength of spirit to vanquish his foe or to die bravely whenever it is necessary to fight for one's childrens's sake, for religion, for one's sacred places, or for the honor and salvation of one's country." These lively arguments adorned with such graceful expression won me over immediately.[13]

As the scholar who recently found this passage, René Graziani, remarks, Wyatt spoke Spanish, and the two may well have conversed in that language, or, I might add, in Latin. But Graziani also notes that the Spanish of the report is uncharacteristically stilted. And he points out that behind Wyatt's remarks here lies a passage attributed to Themistocles in Aelian's *Varia historia*. The passage, an etiology for the yearly cockfight in Athens, reports

Themistocles's praise for a pair of cocks. Their valor is a model for his troops on the eve of battle:

These two Coks endaunger themselues, as we see, to the death, not for their countryes cause, not for the household gods, not for the Priuiledges of their honorable ancestors, not for renown, nor for libertie, not for wife & children: But that th'one might not ouercrowe & beat th'other, or that th'one shoud giue grounde and game to the other, as the worse to the better, the weaker to the stronger, Which words being beutified with the flowers of polisie, minstred marvailous incouragement to the harts of the Athenians, which stoutness and audacitie, he wished and also willed so to be put in practise, that thereby they might purchase perpetuall remembrance.[14]

Graziani thinks it more likely that Wyatt, unbeknownst to Don Andrés, sprang to the defense of the sport with a recollection of this commonplace, shifting its terms slightly to make the point more directly about its usefulness to the republic. I am not so sure. For either or both men could surely have known this story and inserted it into its appropriate rhetorical space. And either could have altered the imitation to make it closer to or further from its source. Who is speaking? Don Andrés de Laguna? Aelian? Themistocles? Sir Thomas Wyatt? My answer would be one or some or all. For Wyatt's identity, like that of Don Andrés, was inscribed in relation to texts he did not write. And our histories, if they are to be true, must be read from stories that we do not fully understand.

Notes and References

Chapter One

1. J. S. Brewer et al., eds., *Letters and Papers, Foreign and Domestic, of the Reign of Henry VIII,* 21 vols. and addenda (London; Her Majesty's Stationers Office, 1862–1932), vol. 2, item 2735; henceforth cited as *LP* by volume and item (i.e., *LP* 2.2735). Kenneth Muir, *Life and Letters of Sir Thomas Wyatt* (Liverpool: Liverpool University Press, 1963), 216.

2. For a description of Egerton MS. 2711, see Richard Harrier, *The Canon of Sir Thomas Wyatt's Poetry* (Cambridge: Harvard University Press, 1975), 1–15.

3. Harrier, *Canon,* 11, claims that the "Tho." is identical to Wyatt's normal signature in his letters; R. A. Rebholz, *Sir Thomas Wyatt, the Complete Poems* (Harmondsworth, England: Penguin, 1978; rpt., New Haven: Yale University Press, 1981), 16, disputes that it is the same hand as Wyatt's in Egerton and suggests that the intimacy of the address by first name suggests someone close to the family. Poems are quoted from Rebholz by poem and line number (i.e., 1.3–7).

4. On the collection of lyrics in the fifteenth and early sixteenth century, see Julia Boffey, *Manuscripts of English Courtly Love Lyrics in the Later Middle Ages* (London: D. S. Brewer, 1985).

5. See Helen V. Baron, "Wyatt's 'What rage,'" *Library,* 5th ser., 31, no. 3 (1975):188–204. Baron uses ultraviolet light to detect different stages of composition.

6. Harrier, *Canon,* 9.

7. The Wyatt letters have been transcribed by Kenneth Muir in *Life and Letters.*

8. Muir, *Life and Letters,* 183.

9. John Bruce, "Unpublished Anecdotes of Sir Thomas Wyatt the Poet, and of Other Members of That Family," *Gentleman's Magazine* 32 (September 1850), 236.

10. George Frederick Nott, ed., *The Works of Henry Howard, Earl of Surrey, and of Sir Thomas Wyatt the Elder,* 2 vols. (London: T. Bensley for Longman, Hurst, Rees, Orme, and Brown, 1815), 1:x–xx. Nott gives several generations of Wyatt genealogy.

11. Bruce, "Anecdotes," 235.

12. On Henry Wyatt's career, see Agnes Conway, *Henry VII's Relations with Scotland and Ireland 1485–1498* (Cambridge: Cambridge University Press, 1932), 7–8, 18–19, 28–30, 34–39, 55–56, 65–69, 83, 100–110.

13. *LP* 1.2053. He was dismissed in November 1513, (*LP* 1.2480).

14. *LP* 2.842.

15. Conway, *Relations,* 68–69; *Calendar of Patent Rolls, Henry VII,* 2 vols. (London: His Majesty's Stationer's Office, 1914), 1:136, 219; 2:16, 27, 219, 237,

367; *Calendar of Close Rolls Henry VII,* 2 vols. (London: Her Majesty's Stationer's Office, 1955–62) 1, item 250.

16. On Wyatt as esquire of the body, see Muriel St. Clare Byrne, *The Lisle Letters* (Chicago: University of Chicago Press), 1:148–49.

17. Muir, *Life and Letters* (3), suggests that Henry Wyatt was knighted for military service at the Battle of the Spurs; he is first listed as knight banneret for the marriage of Princess Mary to Louis XIII in 1514 (*LP* 1.3348).

18. Bruce, "Anecdotes," 237.

19. *LP* 1.81.

20. Muir, *Life and Letters,* 38.

21. Ibid., 3; Nott, *Works,* ii; *LP* 1.54, 438, part 3, m. 10; *LP* 2.699, 4391.

22. There is no record of Wyatt's marriage, but the birth of his eldest son can be backdated from his age at Wyatt's death to 1520.

23. *LP* 12.312, 539, 637, 766.

24. Muir, *Life and Letters,* 39–40.

25. Bruce, "Anecdotes," 239.

26. Muir, *Life and Letters,* 31; *LP* 10.840.

27. Ibid., 35–36.

28. Ibid., 39, 43.

29. *LP* addenda 1.1070; letter from Sir Richard Graynffeld, high marshall of Calais to the king. See also William H. Wiatt, "On the Date of Sir Thomas Wyatt's Knighthood," *Journal of English and Germanic Philology* 40 (1961):268–72.

30. *LP* 11.1492.

31. *LP* 11.580, 1217, 519, 1026.

32. Muir, *Life and Letters,* 3.

33. *LP* 12.312, 539, 637, 766.

34. Muir, *Life and Letters,* 40–41.

35. Ibid., 43.

36. *LP* 2.2735; 4.214.

37. It is frequently said that Wyatt attended St. John's College, the high seat of the new learning. But there is no authority for this assertion, which is no doubt due to documentary confusion of Wyatt with another Wyatt at Cambridge (John Wyatt, M. A., 1520) and to a certain degree of wishful thinking. Leland was not affiliated with St. John's. On the confused documents see John Venn and J. A. Venn, *Alumni Cantabrigienses* (Cambridge: Cambridge University Press), Part 1, 4:480.

38. J. D. Alsop, "The Structure of Early Tudor Finance, ca. 1509–1558," in *Revolution Reassessed,* ed. Christopher Coleman and David Starkey (Oxford: Oxford University Press, 1986), 148.

39. *Calendar of Patent Rolls, Henry VII,* 1.153.

40. *LP* 3.491; 3.2486.

41. *LP* 4.6418, no. 8.

42. *LP* 4.675.

43. *LP* 5.838, no. 13.

44. *LP* 6.601, 701.

45. *LP* 7.674.

46. *LP* 7.922; *LP* 8.249, 275, 349.

47. Wiatt, "On the Date," 269.

48. David Loades, *The Tudor Court* (Totowa, N.J.: Barnes & Noble, 1987), 31.

49. David Starkey, "The Age of the Household: Politics, Society, and the Arts c. 1350–c. 1550," in Stephen Medcalf, ed., *The Later Middle Ages in England* (New York: Holmes and Meier, 1981), 225–90. For a fascinating account of the Henrician court, see Starkey's *The Reign of Henry VIII: Personalities and Politics* (New York: Franklyn Watts, 1986).

50. Alsop, "Structure of Early Tudor Finance," 148.

51. Loades, *Tudor Court*, 79.

52. Ibid., 76. The administration of the household accounts through the Cofferer was placed under the supervision of the treasurer of the chamber in 1523 according to 14 Henry VII, c. 19.

53. Ibid., 82.

54. Ibid., 79.

55. Bruce, "Anecdotes," 237.

56. *LP* 4.2075.

57. *LP* 12.870.

58. *LP* 4.2163.

59. Muir, *Life and Letters*, 150.

60. *LP* 14.63, 71, quoted from the transcription of Patricia Thomson, *Sir Thomas Wyatt and His Background* (Stanford: Stanford University Press, 1964), 46.

61. Muir, *Life and Letters*, 111.

62. Ibid., 161–62.

63. *LP* 4.2194; Muir, *Life and Letters*, 102, see also 98.

64. Ibid., 110.

65. Ibid., 114–15.

66. Ibid., 105.

67. Ibid.

68. Ibid., 100, 145.

69. Ibid., 126.

70. Ibid., 124–25.

71. Ibid., 127.

72. Ibid., 66.

73. Ibid., 65.

74. For a full account of the episode, see Thomas F. Mayer, "A Diet for Henry VIII: The Failure of Reginald Pole's 1537 Legation," *Journal of British Studies* 26 (1987):305–31.

75. *LP* 14.212.

76. Muir, *Life and Letters*, 66.

77. Ibid., 122–23.

78. Ibid., 175–76; *LP* 16.467.

79. *LP* 15.782, 942.

80. Muir, *Life and Letters,* 177.

81. *LP* 16.660, 662.

82. *LP* 17.71, no. 24.

83. *LP* 17.1258.

84. *LP* 17.220.

85. *LP* 17.598.

86. Muir, *Life and Letters,* 216.

87. David Starkey, "The Age of the Household," 278.

88. Pierre Bourdieu, *Outline of a Theory of Practice,* trans. Richard Nice (Cambridge: Cambridge University Press, 1977).

89. *Naeniae in mortem T. Viati, equitis incomparabilis* (London: R. Wolfe, 1542); *STC* 18446. My translations.

90. Henry Howard, *Earl of Surrey, Poems,* ed. Emrys Jones, (Oxford: Oxford University Press, 1964), no. 28.

91. Ibid.

92. Harrier, *Canon,* 7–15.

93. Ibid., 40.

94. Hyder Rollins, ed., *Tottel's Miscellany (1557–1587),* 2 vols. (Cambridge: Harvard University Press, 1928; rev. ed. 1965), 1:2.

Chapter Two

1. British Library 1854–6–28–74. The drawing is widely reproduced; see, for example, Loades, *Tudor Court,* plate 10.

2. *Household Ordinances* (London: Society of Antiquaries, 1790), 153; quoted by Loades, *Tudor Court,* 63.

3. For a recent survey of Holbein's career in England, see *Holbein and the Court of Henry VIII* (London: The Queen's Gallery, Buckingham Palace, 1978).

4. Ibid., 7.

5. On the portrait of Thomas Wyatt, see ibid., 119–21. The portrait I have described is Royal Library 12250, cataloged by K. T. Parker, *The Drawings of Hans Holbein in the Collection of H. M. the King at Windsor Castle* (London: Phaidon Press, 1945), no. 64. The relation between this drawing and a companion drawing (heavily drawn over in black ink) remains in question.

6. Roy Strong, "From Manuscript to Miniature," chapter 2 of John Murdoch, Jim Murrell, Patrick J. Noon and Roy Strong, *The English Miniature* (New Haven: Yale University Press, 1981), 36.

7. An anonymous reviewer of Tillyard's edition of Wyatt in 1929 wrote (oblivious, I suspect, to the fullest implications of his words) that "the mystery of Wyatt is simply whether he knew what he was doing or whether he did not" ([London] *Times Literary Supplement,* 19 September 1929, 709–10).

8. E. W. Ives, *Anne Boleyn* (London: Basil Blackwell, 1986), plate 27 [King's MS 9].

9. Julia Boffey, "The Manuscripts of English Courtly Love Lyrics in the Fifteenth Century," in *Manuscripts and Readers in Fifteenth Century England: The Literary Implications of Manuscript Study,* ed. Derek Pearsall (Cambridge: D. S. Brewer, 1983), 8–9.

10. David Scott, "Wyatt's Worst Poem," (London) *Times Literary Supplement,* 13 September 1963, 696. Scott's argument for this specific occasion is inconclusive, although there would seem no reason to dismiss it as Rebholz does (*Poems,* 490) by taking the reference to war in the unrevised version of line 51 as topical. Scott demonstrates that the poem was based in part on Johannes de Sacrobosco's *de Sphaera.*

11. *Petrarch's Lyric Poems, the Rime Sparse and Other Lyrics,* ed. and trans. Robert M. Durling (Cambridge: Harvard University Press, 1976), no. 269; all quotations and translations of the *Rime* are from this edition.

12. See H. A. Mason, *Humanism and Poetry in the Early Tudor Period,* (London: Routledge and Kegan Paul, 1959), 198.

13. *Chronicle of King Henry VIII of England,* ed. Martin A. Sharpe Hume (London: George Bell & Sons, 1889).

14. Quoted from Harrier, *Canon,* 79. The allusion was first noted by Mason, *Humanism and Poetry,* 197; Mason also notes a transcription of a government proclamation that alludes to Cromwell's scaffold speech (British Library MS Harley 3362, fol. 79r). As Mason observes, these references confirm the sometimes unreliable account of the Spanish chronicle. On Cox's commonplace book, Corpus Christi College Cambridge MS 168, which also contains texts of "Like as the bird" and "Mine own John Poyntz," see Harrier, *Canon,* 78–79.

15. Muir, *Life and Letters,* 66.

16. I have not translated the "V." abbreviation in the Latin; it may stand for "vera," i.e. "true" innocence.

17. C. S. Lewis, *English Literature in the Sixteenth Century Excluding Drama* (Oxford: Oxford University Press, 1954), 230.

18. Boffey, "Manuscripts of Lyrics," 11. For later settings, see, for example, Ivy L. Mumford, "Musical Settings to the Poems of Sir Thomas Wyatt," *Music and Letters* 37 (1956):315–22; "Sir Thomas Wyatt's Songs: A Trio of Problems in Manuscript Sources," *Music and Letters,* 39 (1958):262–64; "Sir Thomas Wyatt's Verse and Italian Musical Sources," *English Miscellany* 14 (1963):9–26; and Winifred Maynard, "The Lyrics of Wyatt: Poems or Songs?" *Review of English Studies,* n.s. 16 (1965):1–13.

19. John Stevens, *Music and Poetry at the Early Tudor Court* (London: Methuen, 1961), 160.

20. Richard C. Harrier, "A Printed Source for the Devonshire Manuscript," *Review of English Studies* n.s. 11 (1960):54; H. A. Mason, "Wyatt and Hercules," *ELH* (1985):213–14; Harrier, *Canon,* 10, 12.

21. See H. A. Mason, "Wyatt among the Muses," *Notes and Queries* 231 (1986):311–12.

22. Stephen Greenblatt, *Renaissance Self-Fashioning* (Chicago: University of Chicago Press, 1980), 152; Thomas Greene, *The Light from Troy: Imitation and Discovery in Renaissance Poetry* (New Haven: Yale University Press, 1982), 242–63.

23. Greenblatt, *Renaissance Self-Fashioning*, 153. Greenblatt is borrowing the phrase "internal distance" from the work of the influential Marxist cultural theorist Louis Althusser.

24. Jones, *Surrey*, 28.13; Leland, *Naeniae*, sig A_2; George Puttenham, *The Arte of English Poesie*, ed. Gladys Doidge Willcock and Alice Walker (Cambridge: Cambridge University Press, 1936), 60.

25. See the valuable survey of Patricia Thomson, "Wyatt and the School of Serafino," in *Sir Thomas Wyatt and His Background*, 209–37.

26. Muir, *Life and Letters*, 167.

27. J. G. Fucilla, "The Direct Source of Wyatt's Epigram: In Dowtfull Brest . . . ," *Renaissance News* 9 (1956):187–88.

28. Muir, *Life and Letters*, 86.

29. *Rime* 180; I have altered Durling's translation slightly to bring out the parallels to Wyatt's poem. Is Durling right in glossing *corno* as "on your horn," i.e., "on the horn" of a mythological river god? Or does "horn" simply mean "crescent"; i.e., is this what Wyatt was translating in "bended moon"?

30. Rollins, *Tottel's Miscellany*, 1:81.

31. H. A. Mason, "Wyatt and Hercules," *English Literary History* 51 (1984):207–18.

Chapter Three

1. Greenblatt, *Renaissance Self-Fashioning*, 131.

2. For convenience I refer to the text of Alamanni in Muir and Thomson, *Collected Poems*, 347 (my translation).

3. There were two contemporaries named John Poyntz (Poins, Pointz): John Poyntz of North Ockenden, Essex, and John Poyntz of Alderley, Gloucestershire, son of Sir Robert Poyntz of Iron Acton. Poyntz of Alderly is the subject of a Holbein drawing; his close connections to the court make him the likelier addressee here. See *Holbein*, 87–88.

4. Muir, *Life and Letters*, 43.

5. Ibid., 40.

6. Nott (2:562) notes the section of Livy recounting the suicide of Cato is lost, but its contents are known from the epitome appended to the histories.

7. Anthony Giddens, *The Constitution of Society: Outline of the Theory of Structuration* (Berkeley: University of California Press, 1985).

8. On Wyatt's use of "ye"/"thee", see Rebholz, *Poems*, 34–35.

9. I have changed Rebholz's punctuation here, since I do not accept his read-

ing of the lines, preferring with Joost Daalder to read "let present pass" in apposition to "to continue your sore." As Daalder says, "as far as sixteenth-century sources of the poem are concerned, Rebholz's punctuation has no more authority than mine; both are guided by what we believe to be the sense, as there is no punctuation to help us in the primary sources on which our editions are based" (*Collected Poems* [London: Oxford University Press, 1975]). In his discussion of the lines (448–49), Rebholz ignores the reference to Plutarch. He offers two interpretations of the last two lines, neither of which makes sense, as he does not comprehend that "Let present pass" in 101 is dependent upon "list" in 100; Wyatt is saying that you are mad if you list to continue your sore, if you let the present pass, if you gape on time to come [instead], and if you [thus] deep your self in travail more and more. See Joost Daalder, "Seneca and Wyatt's Second Satire," *Etudes Anglaises* 38 (1985):422–27.

10. Muir, *Life and Letters*, 42–43.

11. Ibid., 43.

12. Greenblatt, *Renaissance Self-Fashioning*, 135.

13. On Brian as a collector of proverbs, see Rollins, *Tottel's Miscellany*, 2:82.

14. Rebholz loses his usual circumspection when he alleges that because of a disparaging reference Wyatt made to Brian in 1539, this poem must clearly have been written in 1536. Wyatt was still on good terms with Brian in 1541, when he addressed to him a dedicatory poem to the psalms. In the letter Rebholz quotes Wyatt thanks Cromwell for repaying him the money he had lent to Brian, commenting, "If the kings honour more than his credit had not been afore mine eyes, he should have piped an ivy leaf for aught of me" (Muir, *Life and Letters*, 86). Wyatt's complaint is jocular. He suggests that Brian was a bad credit risk and that he lent him the money only because Brian (like Wyatt) himself was on the king's service so that the money was in effect guaranteed by the crown.

15. Muir, *Life and Letters*, 181.

16. Ibid., 67.

17. Ibid., 199.

18. Ibid., 197.

19. Muir, *Life and Letters*, 198.

20. Nott suggests the reference is to Sir Thomas Kitson, sheriff of London in 1533; he is supported by Raymond Southall, who also explains the reference to giving cheese to a dog ("Wyatt and Kytson," *Notes and Queries* 219, n.s. 21, no. 11 [November]:403–4). Rollins (*Tottel's Miscellany*, 2:82) argues plausibly for the rich London bookseller Antony Kitson.

Chapter Four

1. *LP* 4.297, no. 1.

2. *LP* 6.2.45.

3. Thomas Wright, *Three Chapters of Letters Relating to the Suppression of Monasteries* (London: Camden Society Publications, 1843), no. 26, 59–60.

4. Muir, *Life and Letters*, 195–196, 204.

5. Thomas More, *A Dialogue Concerning Heresies,* ed. Thomas M. C. Lawler et al., vol. 6, *Yale Edition of the Complete Works of St. Thomas More* (New Haven: Yale University Press, 1981), 88. I have altered the punctuation slightly.

6. Ives, *Anne Boleyn,* plate 30, said to be from "Sotheby and Co."

7. Rebholz, *Poems,* 455, carefully sorts out the arguments and concludes "a precise dating of the psalms seems to me impossible." On Wyatt's sources, see 452–55.

8. Alexandra Halasz, "Wyatt's David," *English Literary History* (1987):331.

9. Ibid., 332.

10. George Watson, *The English Petrarchans: A Critical Bibliography of the Canzoniere* (London: Warburg Institute, 1967), 3.

11. Greene, *Light in Troy.*

12. See Muir and Thomson, *Collected Poems,* 264.

13. *Lisle Letters,* 4:46.

14. Ives, *Anne Boleyn,* 277.

15. Ibid., plate 27 [King's MS 9].

16. C. E. Nelson, "A Note on Wyatt and Ovid," *Modern Language Review* 58 (1963):60–63.

Postscript

1. On Tottel and the editions of his miscellany, see Rollins, *Tottel's Miscellany,* 1:2.

2. See ibid.

3. Gladys Willcock and Alice Walker, eds., *The Arte of English Poesie* (Cambridge: Cambridge University Press, 1936), 62.

4. Willmarth Lewis et al., eds., *Horace Walpole's Correspondence* (New Haven: Yale University Press, 1937–83), 41:320–21.

5. Lewis, *Horace Walpole's Correspondence,* 28:6.

6. Thomas Warton, *History of English Poetry* (London: J. Dodsley et al., 1774), 3:27.

7. *Letters of Mary Wollstonecraft Shelley,* ed. Betty T. Bennett (Baltimore: Johns Hopkins University Press, 1980), 1:223; see also 1:214; *Journals of Mary Shelley 1814–1844,* ed. Paula R. Feldman and Diana Scott-Kilvert (Oxford: Oxford University Press, 1987), 1:386, 400.

8. John Bruce, "Recovery of the Lost Accusation of Sir Thomas Wyatt the Poet by Bishop Bonner," *Gentleman's Magazine* 32 (1850), 563–70.

9. See, for example, Rudolf Alscher, *Sir Thomas Wyatt und Seine Stellung in der Entwickelungeschicte der Englischen Literatur und Verkunst,* Weiner Beitrage zur Deutschen und Englischen Philologie (Vienna: Wilhelm Braumuller, 1886) Agnes Foxwell, *A Study of Sir Thomas Wyatt's Poems* (London: University of London Press, 1911); *The Poems of Sir Thomas Wyatt* (London: University of London Press, 1913); William Simonds, *Sir Thomas Wyatt and His Poems* (Boston: D.C. Heath, 1889);

and Egon Wintermantel, *Biographisches in den Gedichten von Sir Thomas Wyatt and Henry Howard, Earl of Surrey,* (Furtwangen: Wilhelm Kirchberg, 1903).

10. Works mentioned in the following paragraphs are listed in the Selected Bibliography.

11. Eleanor Hammond, "Poems 'Signed' by Sir Thomas Wyatt," *Modern Language Notes* 37 (1922):505–6.

12. Ethel Seaton, "The 'Wyatt,' 'Surrey,' and Tottel Poems," in *Sir Richard Roos, c. 1410–1482, Lancastrian Poet* (London: Rupert Hart-Davis, 1961), 454–519.

13. René Graziani, "Sir Thomas Wyatt at a Cockfight," *Review of English Studies,* n.s. 27 (1976):301–3. The translations from Laguna are Graziani's.

14. Aelian, *Varia historia* 2:28, trans. Abraham Fleming, *A Register of Hystories* (London, 1576), fol. 22; quoted by Graziani, 303.

Selected Bibliography

PRIMARY WORKS

Manuscripts

British Library, Egerton MS. 2711. Wyatt's personal manuscript.
British Library, Harley MS. 282. Wyatt's Letters.
British Library, Add. MS. 17492. A courtly miscellany of the 1530s and 1540s; passed on by successive dukes of Devonshire.
Arundel-Harington MS. Owned by the duke of Norfolk (Arundel Castle MS [Special Press]). Sixteenth-century miscellany in the family of Sir John Harrington of Stepney.
Blage MS. Trinity College, Dublin, MS. 160. Miscellany owned by Wyatt's acquaintance Sir George Blage.

Editions and Textual Studies

Baron, Helen V. "Wyatt's 'What rage.'" *Library,* 5th ser., no. 3 (September): 188–204. Ultraviolet examination of the Egerton version shows Wyatt revising with different inks in three possible stages of composition.
————. "Sir Thomas Wyatt's Seven Penitential Psalms: A Study of Textual and Source Materials." Ph.D. diss., Cambridge University, 1977. Fresh study of textual problems.
Daalder, Joost, ed. *Sir Thomas Wyatt, Collected Poems.* London: Oxford University Press, 1975. Modern spelling; separates poems by manuscripts in which they appear.
Foxwell, Agnes. *The Poetry of Sir Thomas Wiat.* 2 vols. London: University of London Press, 1913. An important early edition.
Harrier, Richard C., ed. *The Canon of Thomas Wyatt's Poetry.* Cambridge: Harvard University Press, 1975. Diplomatic transcription of Egerton MS. 2711 with variants from other sources; full study of all textual sources and of problems of canon.
Hughey, Ruth. *The Arundel Harington Manuscript of Tudor Poetry.* 2 vols. Columbus: Ohio State University Press, 1960. Useful commentary and textual remarks.
Mason, H. A. *Editing Wyatt: An Examination of "Collected Poems of Sir Thomas Wyatt" Together with Suggestions for an Improved Edition.* Cambridge:

Cambridge Quarterly, 1972. Identifies hundreds of errors in transcription of Muir and Thomson edition; calls for edition with an eclectic text.

————. *Sir Thomas Wyatt, A Literary Portrait*. Bristol: Bristol Classical Press, 1986. Selected poems with running commentary.

Muir, Kenneth, ed. *Sir Thomas Wyatt and His Circle, Unpublished Poems*. Transcribes the Blage Manuscript. Doubtful remarks about canon.

Muir, Kenneth and Patricia Thomson, eds. *Collected Poems of Sir Thomas Wyatt*. Liverpool: Liverpool University Press, 1969. Text contains errors in transcription; discussion of canon undiscriminating; commentary useful; often prints full versions of sources.

Nott, G. F., ed. *The Works of Henry Howard, Earl of Surrey, and of Sir Thomas Wyatt the Elder*. 2 vols. London: T. Bensley for Hurst, Rees, Orme, and Brown, 1815–16. Introduction and commentary still useful, especially on family history and sources; Wyatt's works in vol. 2.

Rebholz, R. A., ed. *Sir Thomas Wyatt: The Complete Poems*. Harmondsworth: Penguin, 1978; rpt., New Haven: Yale University Press, 1981. Modern spelling; separates poems by form; superb commentary and perceptive study of problems of canon.

Rollins, Hyder E., ed. *Tottel's Miscellany (1557–1587)*, 2 vols. Cambridge: Harvard University Press, 1928; 2d ed., 1965. Excellent commentary.

Tillyard, E. M. W. *The Poetry of Sir Thomas Wyatt: A Selection and a Study*. London: Scholartis Press, 1929. Established Wyatt's prominence in the modern literary canon.

SECONDARY WORKS

Bibliography and Reference

Hengen, E. C. *A Concordance to the Complete Poetical Works of Sir Thomas Wyatt*. Chicago: University of Chicago Press, 1941.

Jentoft, Clyde W. *Sir Thomas Wyatt and Henry Howard, Earl of Surrey, A Reference Guide*. Boston: G. K. Hall, 1980. Bibliography to 1978.

Biography

Bruce, John. "Unpublished Anecdotes of Sir Thomas Wyatt the Poet, and of Other Members of That Family." *Gentleman's Magazine* 32 (September 1850), 235–41. Stories from the Wyatt family manuscript.

Loades, D. M. ed. *The Papers of George Wyatt Esquire of Boxley Abbey in the County of Kent, Son and Heir of Sir Thomas Wyatt the Younger*. Camden Society 4th series, no. 5. London: Camden Society, 1967. Describes Wyatt family manuscripts.

Muir, Kenneth. *Sir Thomas Wyatt, Life and Letters.* Liverpool: Liverpool University Press, 1963. Prints texts of Wyatt's letters.

Tydeman, W. M. "Biographical Data on Sir Thomas Wyatt." *Notes and Queries* 7 (1961): 414–15. Corrects some problems of dating.

Wiatt, William H. "On the Date of Sir Thomas Wyatt's Knighthood." *Journal of English and Germanic Philology* 40 (1961):268–72.

Literary and Historical Studies

Baldi, Sergio. *La poesia di Sir Thomas Wyatt, il primo petrarchista Inglese.* Florence: Le Monnier, 1953. Excellent remarks about the introduction of a neoclassicizing caesura in Wyatt's metrics.

————. *Sir Thomas Wyatt.* Translated by F. T. Prince. London: Longmans, 1961. A brief interpretation.

Buxton, John. *A Tradition of Poetry.* London: Macmillan, 1961. Sees Wyatt as English gentleman and international courtier.

Chambers, E. K. *Sir Thomas Wyatt and Some Collected Studies.* London: Sidgwick and Jackson, 1933. Says Wyatt is best at "lyrical" ballads in medieval tradition. Biographical data on Elizabeth Darrell.

Estrin, Barbara. "Becoming the Other/the Other Becoming in Wyatt's Poetry" *English Literary History* 51 (1984):431–45. Dense and rich study of rhetorical slippage of Wyatt's persona.

Friedman, D. M. "The 'Thing' in Wyatt's Mind." *Essays in Criticism* 16 (1966): 375–81. Studies Wyatt's stoic inward turning.

Greenblatt, Stephen. *Renaissance Self-Fashioning.* Chicago: University of Chicago Press, 1980. Contains an influential chapter on Wyatt that explores a poetics of power, inwardness, and sexuality.

Greene, Thomas. *The Light from Troy: Imitation and Discovery in Renaissance Poetry.* New Haven: Yale University Press, 1982. Contains a seminal chapter on Wyatt that discusses his "heuristic" appropriation of classical and continental sources.

Halasz, Alexandra. "Wyatt's David." *English Literary History* (1987):331. A brilliant new reading of the psalms.

Kamholtz, Jonathan Z. "Thomas Wyatt's Poetry: The Politics of Love." *Criticism.* 20 (1978):349–65. Addresses poetry and courtly games of power.

Kerrigan, John. "Wyatt's Selfish Style." *Essays and Studies.* 34 (1981):1–18.

Lewis, C. S. *English Literature in the Sixteenth Century Excluding Drama.* Oxford: Oxford University Press, 1954.

Mason, H. A. *Humanism and Poetry in the Early Tudor Period.* London: Routledge and Kegan Paul, 1959. Addresses Wyatt and the humanist problem of translation.

McManles, Michael. "Love and Power in the Poetry of Sir Thomas Wyatt." *Modern Language Quarterly* 29 (1968):145–60. Examines paradoxical psychological movements in Wyatt's erotic poems.

Panja, Shormistha. "Ranging and Returning: The Mood-Voice Dichotomy in Wyatt." *English Literary Renaissance* 18 (1988):347–68. Posits Wyatt's doubleness as manifestation of a resilient Tudor humanism.

Southall, Raymond. *The Courtly Maker, An Essay on the Poetry of Wyatt and His Contemporaries.* New York: Barnes and Noble, 1964. Examines Wyatt in the context of the courtly manuscripts; studies circulation of Devonshire MS.

Starkey, David. "The Age of the Household: Politics, Society, and the Arts c. 1350–c. 1550." In *The Later Middle Ages in England,* edited by Stephen Medcalf, 225–90. New York: Holmes and Meier, 1981. Excellent material on the structure of the Tudor household.

Stein, Arnold. "Wyatt's 'They flee from me'." *Sewanee Review* 47 (1959):28–44. A classic New Critical reading.

Stevens, John. *Music and Poetry at the Early Tudor Court.* London: Methuen, 1961. Studies Wyatt's relation to the lyric.

Thomson, Patricia. *Sir Thomas Wyatt and His Background.* Stanford: Stanford University Press, 1964. Focuses on Wyatt's biographical and literary background.

Winters, Ivor. "The Sixteenth Century Lyric in England: A Critical and Historical Reinterpretation." *Poetry* 53 (1939):258–72, 320–22. Examines Wyatt and a school of "plain style" poetry in relation to an aureate school.

Wright, George T. "Wyatt's Decasyllabic Line." *Studies in Philology* 82 (1985): 129–56. Uses current theories of prosody.

Index